Cambridge Handbooks for Teachers

GENERAL EDITOR: S. S. F. FLETCHER, M.A.

VIA NOVA

VIA NOVA

OR

THE APPLICATION OF THE DIRECT METHOD TO LATIN AND GREEK

BY

W. H. S. JONES, M.A.
Fellow and Lecturer of St Catharine's College
Lecturer at the Training College for Schoolmasters
Senior Classical Master at the Perse School
Cambridge

Cambridge:
at the University Press
1915

CAMBRIDGE UNIVERSITY PRESS
Cambridge, New York, Melbourne, Madrid, Cape Town,
Singapore, São Paulo, Delhi, Mexico City

Cambridge University Press
The Edinburgh Building, Cambridge CB2 8RU, UK

Published in the United States of America by Cambridge University Press, New York

www.cambridge.org
Information on this title: www.cambridge.org/9781107623149

First published 1915
First paperback edition 2013

A catalogue record for this publication is available from the British Library

ISBN 978-1-107-62314-9 Paperback

W. H. D. R.

COLLEGAE SOCIO AMICO

VTRIVSQVE LINGVAE SERMONES DOCTO

VIAE NOVAE

INVENTORI STRENVOQVE DEFENSORI

HVNC LIBELLVM

D. D. D.

AVCTOR

GENERAL EDITOR'S PREFACE

RECENT years have witnessed a remarkable activity in the educational world, and everywhere we meet with a great effort to make our schools more efficient. Not the least active of the various bodies who are working to achieve this greater efficiency are the teachers themselves. In all the various schools we find teachers eager to keep abreast with the times and striving hard to make themselves more perfect in their particular work. The teaching of the various subjects in the curriculum is engaging the attention of various specialist-teachers, and, as a result, great changes both in curriculum and in methods of teaching are taking place. The self-complacency of the old schoolmaster is vanishing. The place of each separate subject in the curriculum has to be justified. Attempts are being made to find more rational and more scientific reasons than mere tradition for the order in which, and the methods by which, the various parts of a subject should be taught, what parts should be included or omitted and the grounds for their inclusion or omission.

As a result there is a growing desire on the part of teachers, especially the young teachers, to acquaint themselves with the results of these various attempts, and to get information which will be of real assistance to them in their work in the class-room. The present series is intended to meet this demand. The various volumes which will appear in the series of *Cambridge Handbooks for Teachers* will be written by experienced teachers, each of whom has for a considerable time been working out the problem how his particular subject can best be taught, and each of whom has tested his theories by practical application in the class-room. Each volume will deal with the scope and purpose of its particular subject, the curriculum, schemes of work, method, equipment and reference-books, in fact with everything which may be helpful to the teachers and assist them in teaching their subjects intelligently.

S. S. F. FLETCHER.

January, 1915.

PREFACE

THE arguments against a classical education have often struck me as forcible and persuasive. At the same time the conviction has never left me that a training in classics is a good thing for those who can profit thereby, and that if the "direct method" be adopted and intelligently applied the number of such is greatly increased, while the standard of attainment is considerably raised. Accordingly I have attempted to describe what the direct method is, and how it can be adapted to Latin and Greek.

But the ultimate fate of the classical curriculum will not be determined by discussion; I doubt whether argument has ever made a convert of an opponent. The support of parents can be won only by results. If it be felt that our boys and girls are made fitter for life—for its duties, its drudgery and its relaxations—then, and then only, will the battle be decided in favour of one curriculum or another.

Teachers of classics, therefore, have a difficult task before them. They must remember that their subject has lost the almost superstitious respect in which it was once held, and that it now stands upon its own merits. They must rely upon no argument save that of results, abandon the useless weapons of debate and discussion, and concentrate all their energies upon the really useful task of seeking the good of the young lives committed to their charge.

I do not attempt to make converts. This little book is addressed to such teachers as are already persuaded that a classical training is a good thing, and are not unduly prejudiced against the direct method. And I would ask them to remember that this method has been practised as yet in only a few schools, so that what I have to say consists mainly of testimony derived from the personal experience of myself and of my friends. I trust that this necessary character of my exposition will not be ascribed to egotism.

The specimen lessons are printed as given, whenever possible, with all their imperfections upon them. It is difficult for the master always to avoid errors in oral work, but the effect upon the class is evanescent, experience proving that the boys suffer no permanent, if any, harm, provided that the master takes pains to improve.

To my colleagues, especially to Dr W. H. D. Rouse and Mr R. B. Appleton, I am so indebted that I cannot repay them by any formal acknowledgment. The latter prepared and gave most of the specimen lessons in chapter v.

Probably no written account—certainly no words of mine—can give a true description of the New Way to the old world. Something, however, of the spirit animating the pilgrims who travel along it can perhaps be felt in the verses at the end of *Initium*.

Hic meus liber, o puer
qui studes sapientiae,
si placet tibi, dum docet,
si docet, tibi dum placet,
munus omne peregit.

scripta pagina fabulas,
picta pagina imagines,
pagina omnis habet iocos;
mixta seria cum iocis
taedium grave tollunt.

disce grammaticam, puer;
civis, indue te toga;
Caesarem gladio neca,
Brute, cum sociis tuis;
tu renascere, Roma!

Roma militibus potens,
Roma legibus utilis,
Roma Vergilii parens,
virtutis pueris dedit,
dat, dabit documentum.

W. H. S. J.

October, 1915.

CONTENTS

CHAPTER I

THE DIRECT METHOD

Many people are certain to regard a book on the teaching of classics as almost an impertinence. If there is any well-beaten track in education, it is surely here. Thousands of teachers have followed it for generations; an elaborate system has been worked out; text-books for at least fifty years have exhibited a uniformity broken only by slight and unimportant variations. Although for about two hundred years (approximately 1500–1700) the methods of teaching classics were keenly discussed, there followed a period of comparative quiet, during which the tradition was subjected to but few attacks.

About twelve years ago, however, there arose a school of teachers who began to urge that the critics of a classical curriculum, who had been rapidly increasing both in numbers and in importance, were really assailing the wrong enemy; that they ought to have attacked, not the subject, but current methods of teaching it. The school has now several supporters, while its many enemies in the main belong to one or the other of two classes. There are, in the first place, teachers of the old school who object to the proposed change just because it is a change; convinced that a classical education is a good thing, they are unwilling to run any risks of impairing its efficacy by adopting any radical alteration of method. There are others who dislike a classical education, or who think it unsuitable for the great majority of boys in secondary schools. The latter class of opponents often admit that the changes are an improvement in method, but they are for this very reason all the more opposed to them. If the end be bad, they argue, the more efficacious the method of reaching that end the more strenuously it ought to be opposed as a pernicious and dangerous thing. It is therefore obvious that an explanation of the new method necessitates a full statement of the aims and principles which underlie it. Let us first consider the question historically.

It will be generally admitted that down to the eighteenth century there was an intimate relation between the classical languages, particularly Latin, and life. A man was excluded from a knowledge of nearly all professional or humanistic subjects unless he could understand the books in which such subjects were treated, and these were, with few exceptions, the Latin and Greek classics and the current Latin literature. Latin was the language of the Church, medicine, law, science, mathematics and scholarship. Accordingly, the study of Latin in schools as a propaedeutic was a necessity that nobody ever dreamed of disputing. Furthermore, there was little need for the inclusion of any other subject in the curriculum of young boys, and, as they grew older, their study of Latin was maintained by reading treatises on special subjects written in that language. A boy's theses, exercises, and often his conversations in school were generally in Latin, which was the language in which he was expected to express his own thoughts, feelings and ideas. In consequence there was a unity in the old curriculum which is entirely wanting in the amorphous mass of subjects which now goes by that name. The old curriculum ought to be compared, not with a modern school course, but with the course of a classical honours student at the University, which includes composition, grammar, literature and many other branches of learning, differing from one another but intimately related.

But the eighteenth century witnessed a great change, which was completed in the nineteenth. Modern languages became the medium in which learned or professional men expressed themselves, and Latin gradually ceased to be a common means of intercourse, until it survived only in the Roman Church, among scholars, and, to a very limited extent, among lawyers. In this way Latin was divorced from common life, but it continued to be studied in schools as a "mental gymnastic" and as the key to a humanising literature. Greek also, which had never been a living language in the Western world as Latin long continued to be, ceased to be of much use to professional men, as the substance of the works of Aristotle, Hippocrates and Galen was transfused into modern literatures.

Broadly speaking, the history of classical study diverges in two directions from about the time of the French Revolution. In Germany the scientific side was developed, in England the artistic side. On the one hand, there are diligent inquiries in the regions of philology, history, philosophy and archaeology; on the other hand we have the cult of the "elegant scholar," who regarded a false quantity or a clumsy phrase as almost a moral blemish. In Germany, the supreme test of attainment came to be the writing of a thesis on some more or less important point in classical antiquities; in England, the examination system had a very powerful influence upon the methods of teaching. It is the tendency of examiners to ask questions that are easily corrected, and translation from one language to another lends itself readily to this purpose. So true is this, that translation papers from English into Latin or Greek are actually called exercises in composition, although strictly speaking they involve no composition—that is, no self-expression—at all, but merely a transference of another man's thoughts from one language to another. In fact, the more thoroughly a candidate eliminates his own thoughts when doing such a piece of translation the more faithfully he does his work. A passage of Shakespeare is best rendered into Greek Iambics when the translator suppresses his own personality and tries to write as Sophocles or Euripides would have written. The translator's mind must not be creative.

The demand for translation in higher examinations has affected methods of teaching down to the beginners' stage. The consequence is, that right through his course the learner of classics is concerned with finding equivalents in one language for words of another, and there is a strong tendency for him to forget or to overlook the realities for which these words stand. The truth of this statement is manifest upon the inspection of almost any batch of papers sent up at public examinations. A large percentage of candidates will be found who have written sheer nonsense, having failed to realise that anything is necessary except to find words to represent other words. Moreover, it may well be doubted whether translation is a good instrument of education before the learner's mind is alive to its serious difficulties. Very few words in any language have exact equivalents in any other; so much of the force of a word depends upon its traditional associations. "Friend" in English and φίλος in Greek afford a typical example. Of course when an advanced scholar, aware of these difficulties, undertakes a piece of translation, he is engaged on an exercise at once profitable and enjoyable; but to allow a beginner to do little else but substitute one expression for another throughout the course of his school life, before his mind can appreciate the necessary imperfection of the results he obtains, is to train him in inaccurate reasoning, and to make him divorce language from the realities it represents.

There is, at any rate, a general dissatisfaction with the results of a classical education. It is said that those who achieve success are often narrow in mind and mechanical in their modes of thought, and, what is worse, the number of failures, who learn practically nothing and cordially detest the little that they do know, is far too great to justify the continuance of the subject in the curriculum of an ordinary school of the secondary type.

Supporters of the reformed method admit that there is much truth in this charge, but they are convinced that most of the fault lies with the present method of treating words apart from the things of which words are mere symbols. Accordingly they would keep Latin for many boys and Greek for a select few, and they would substitute for translation direct association of words with things during the earlier stages at least, and to a certain extent also in the later stages. They rely upon two impulses, which they endeavour carefully to develop, the impulse to understand and the impulse to express one's own thoughts. If by this means a learner of ordinary ability can be trained to appreciate a few classical masterpieces, not only their contents but also the beauty and power of the language in which they are written; if, at the same time, he can learn to express himself in a language that is unrivalled for business-like precision and lucidity, a language, moreover, which will form the basis of his linguistic studies, uniting them into an organised whole, then, and perhaps only then, can Latin and Greek claim an honourable place in a liberal education.

What position in the curriculum should Latin and Greek occupy? Latin must be considered apart from the sister tongue, because few, if any, maintain at the present time that the two tongues are so indissolubly connected that one is useless without the other. Reformers would retain Latin for such boys as will study at least two other foreign languages in the course of their career, in fact for those whose education will be in the main literary. Not only is it important that such boys should have a knowledge of ancient life and thought, but the Latin language itself forms the best possible focus round which linguistic studies can arrange themselves. A language so lucid, precise and business-like has no rival as a means of inculcating those principles of language with which every linguist must be familiar. The mother tongue, at any rate English, though it may teach the simpler elements of general grammar, is not sufficient by itself. A language is required in which the ordinary grammatical categories are clearly marked, and for this purpose Latin is unrivalled. Latin, then, is to be studied primarily for its linguistic value, and secondarily for the content of its best literature. Greek, on the other hand, will be reserved for those few boys who have distinct literary tastes, and the linguistic training afforded by Latin should be employed in securing a rapid and easy mastery of the other language.

The question may also be regarded from another point of view. Reformers look upon education as the placing of a pupil in a series of environments, so as to stimulate the mind to react, and therefore to grow. Contact with the great things of the world, the great facts of nature, and the great achievements of man, is their ultimate aim. The ancient classical literatures, ancient history and civilisation, together with the Latin and Greek tongues, are undoubtedly among the great things of the world, and a knowledge of them is the key to much of our modern life and thought.

A formulation of the reformers' principles must now be given. They base their methods upon the two impulses already mentioned, the impulse to *understand*, and the impulse towards *self-expression*. They desire their lessons to satisfy a real want in their pupils' minds, namely, the wish to express themselves and the wish to understand the thoughts of others. Interest in the work is thus fundamental. This does not mean that hard work is eliminated, but merely that hard work ceases to be drudgery and becomes a pleasure when it happens to be the only means of attaining the desired end. The young learner, then, must not regard his work as a dreary wilderness far removed from the pleasant garden of his own imagination. In the second place, reformers remember that all languages are *tongues*, and that much of their force is lost when they cease to be spoken. This is especially true of Latin and Greek, for most of the great classical authors intended their works to be heard rather than read privately in the study. Oral work, then, plays a large part in the "direct method." Finally, translation as a means of learning a language is abandoned, in order to bring about the direct association of words with reality. Translation, however, still has a part to play. In the earlier stages it is used as a test, to find out whether fresh knowledge has been assimilated; in the later stages it is practised as a literary exercise.

It will be seen that the direct method utilises all the means by which knowledge can reach the brain. It trains not only eyes, but ears and vocal organs. The important part played by the last in mental development has been but recently emphasised by physiologists.

The direct method is not to be identified with the "picking up" or even the neglect of grammar. It is not, or need not be, unsystematic. These points will be dealt with in the following chapters; in the meantime it will be enough to correct a common misconception.

In 1911 and 1912 there were held at Bangor "summer schools" for the reform of Latin teaching, which resulted in the formation of an Association for that purpose. This association appointed a committee to frame a definition of the direct method, and to consider in particular its application to Latin. The report is here reprinted, with the kind permission of the Editor of *Latin Teaching*.

REPORT TO THE ASSOCIATION FOR THE REFORM OF LATIN TEACHING OF THE COMMITTEE APPOINTED TO DEFINE "THE DIRECT METHOD."

We have been asked to attempt a definition of the Direct Method with a view to helping discussions in which the term is used in connexion with the teaching of Latin.

In undertaking such a definition, we were faced by two preliminary questions, (1) the relation of the term "direct" to other terms sometimes used, such as "natural" and "oral," (2) the method of reaching a definition, whether by deduction from first principles or by a Socratic induction from the common use of the term.

USE OF THE TERMS "NATURAL," "ORAL," AND "DIRECT."

In the earlier advocacy of a change in the methods of teaching modern languages the terms "natural" and "oral" are frequently used; their gradual abandonment in favour of the term "direct" seems to be largely due to certain misunderstandings to which they were liable.

The term "natural" was intended to suggest that the pupil should acquire a foreign language in much the same manner as he acquired his own vernacular. But it was soon apparent that the phrase "the natural method" laid itself open to a telling retort by the opponents of change, viz., that the way in which a child learns his mother-tongue is not by a method but by the absence of method. The reformers were fully aware that they could never reproduce in the class-rooms the exact conditions under which a child learns his own language, that the only way he could learn a foreign language "naturally" was by staying in the country in which it is spoken. As the French Circular of 1901 puts it, "while it [the direct method] approximates very nearly to the natural means of acquiring a language, it must be used as a true method, that is to say, in accordance with a definite and graduated plan."

The term "oral" brought out one important element in the proposed changes, but it needed constant explanation. The circular just quoted is obliged to explain: "the oral method does not exclude the reading of texts or written exercises; nor does it rest in abeyance during such exercises: on the contrary, it is to be applied to them."

Eventually the term "direct" was adopted in England to express an attribute applicable throughout, the absence of any "indirect" approach through the medium of the vernacular. It seems less open to objection than the French term "intuitive," which implies the absence of any conscious process of reasoning in reading the correct form, and therefore raises some difficult psychological problems on which we shall touch later.

Method of reaching a Definition.

Though we have stated the original intention of the authors of the term "direct," it may be reasonably maintained that its meaning is much less self-evident than that of the terms "natural," "oral" and "intuitive," and that, whatever it may mean etymologically, it now means just what it is commonly used by its exponents to mean and no more. This leads us to our second preliminary point, the means which we are to employ to reach a definition.

If we could assume in starting that supporters and opponents of the direct method had the same end in view, and that the methods of each were only rival means of securing that end, we should unhesitatingly say that the meaning could be determined solely by the use. But, if adherence or opposition to the method is or can be determined by differences of opinion as to the end in view, or if either party is vague as to its end, then even if the question of the end has not been prominently brought into view in the discussions on the teaching of modern languages, it appears possible that it may suddenly be found to assume a very important place in the controversy as to the application of the method to a new subject-matter, where certain tacit assumptions which may have been made in the case of modern languages may be explicitly called in question.

Questions as to the Aim of the Direct Method.

We feel that our report will be of little value to the Association if we attempt to pass lightly over controversial points; that, if suppressed, they are bound in some form or other to crop up again, and that they had best be faced at the outset.

It is not merely an allegation made by the opponents of the application of the direct method to the teaching of Latin, but an assertion which was once frequently made by upholders of the direct method in its application to modern languages, that the reason for teaching a language orally was because it was to be used orally. This reason could obviously apply only to a modern spoken language. It is further alleged that the method is based on a utilitarian aim, and is opposed to the view which regards a language as a medium of culture. Both these opinions can be supported by the words of the French Ministerial Circular to which reference has already been made. "If the essential object of the study of ancient languages is a certain mental culture, modern languages are taught chiefly with a view to their practical use." "A modern language being in the first place a spoken language, the quickest and most certain method of obtaining a mastery of that language is the oral method."

Further reflexion, however, will show that these considerations are altogether separable from the immediate aim. If it be granted that the "quickest and most certain method of obtaining a mastery of a language is the direct method," no one would feel bound to adopt a slower or more uncertain method because the language was not a spoken language. If a certain mastery of a language is necessary before its value for culture is available, the fact that we seek to master it for purposes of culture and not for utilitarian reasons will not make us less anxious to make progress. When we find the circular going on to state that "Literature, being an essential manifestation of the life of nations, naturally has its place in the teaching of modern languages," even though it hastens to add that it is a subordinate place, when we discover that the later circular of 1902 omits the appeal to utilitarian motives, and when we read in a report on the direct method in Germany amongst eight leading characteristics that the "teaching of the life, customs and institutions, geography, history and literature of the foreign country" is there one of the characteristics of the direct as opposed to the older methods, we may safely come to the conclusion that the utilitarian appeal at any rate was made rather to win over a large section of likely supporters than because it is of the essence of the change. Just as the preamble of an Act of Parliament is immaterial to its provisions, so the ulterior aims alleged by certain supporters of a method cannot be held to override its actual effect.

If, however, we take the French Minister's statement that the direct method is the "quickest and most certain method of obtaining a mastery of a language," we have an immediate reason for its adoption on which we believe that all its adherents are agreed.

We are not called on to prove that the direct method actually is the quickest and most certain method. It may be necessary, however, to point out that the claim may be held by some to be a reason against its adoption. It may be contended that the value of learning a language rests, not primarily in the use which is made of it, whether for purposes of culture or for utilitarian ends, but in the mental training obtained in the process of learning it. The maintenance of such a view is therefore inconsistent with a support of the direct method. No other aim appears to be so.

UNDERLYING PSYCHOLOGICAL ASSUMPTIONS.

Granting that the direct method is advocated on the ground of its supposed speed and certainty, we have still to face the fact that the term is commonly used to cover a considerable number of changes; and it is desirable to see whether its exponents are agreed as to any broad principle from which the desirability of these changes can be inferred; in other words, on any characteristic from which its speed and certainty can be derived. It may be said with confidence that there is a general agreement that such a principle is to be found in its "approximation to the natural means" by which a child learns its mother-tongue. Some analysis of the degree of approximation is therefore necessary.

It is hardly ever now contended that the class-room can completely reproduce the conditions under which a child learns his own language, or even those under which he learns a foreign language in the country where it is spoken. An essential factor in these cases is that during the whole period of learning he practically hears nothing but the new language.

The fundamental fact is that we think in language as well as express our thoughts by that medium. When we speak fluently, thought and speech are almost simultaneous; we are virtually thinking aloud. It is true that, before the words come from our lips or ring on our "mind's ear," some vague notion of what we are thinking about or wish to say must already exist; but this notion is something altogether intangible, it only realises itself as conscious thought when words spring into our mind to give it substance. The words in which we think always tend to be those of our mother-tongue. The complete exception is to be found in a bi-lingual individual living in a bi-lingual environment; conditions may be such as to establish a complete equipoise between two languages, and he thinks in either according to his immediate surroundings or the immediate topic. Persons who speak the language of two or more countries fluently find that they begin normally to think in the language of the country in which they are living after several days' stay in it. Up to that point, it is not that the power of thinking in that language is lacking but that the new vocabulary is *inhibited* by the ready occurrence of the rival vocabulary. The two habits, say of thinking in English and thinking in French, are naturally incompatible. But a slight change in the conditions may reverse the strength of the rival tendencies; the individual who for several days, when he is alone, is thinking in English, may think in French when he is talking to a Frenchman.

A method is therefore direct in so far as it secures that the pupil thinks in the language which he is studying.

This thinking in the new language may obviously vary in amount to any extent. During the French "period" in an English school, it is on the one hand highly improbable that any pupil has succeeded in banishing English entirely from his casual thinking; on the other hand the very beginner is thinking in French when he answers a question promptly in that language or even carries out automatically an order given in that language.

From this it might appear that direct and indirect methods could be mixed in any proportion. But here we have to keep in mind what was said above about inhibition. The natural tendency to think in English is so strong that it is only kept in check by a strong set of mind in the contrary direction. The habit of thinking in French during the French lesson must be so strongly established that this set of mind is automatically established as soon as the lesson begins. Every percentage of English spoken in the lesson will therefore produce a larger percentage of English thought. We would imagine some such scale as the following; it is of course purely imaginary, as the amount of English thought could not possibly be determined; 99 per cent. of French spoken might produce 90 per cent. thought, 90 per cent. might produce 80 per cent., 80 per cent. might produce 50 per cent., 70 per cent. might produce 20 per cent., 60 per cent. might produce 5 per cent., and 50 per cent. might produce 0. We put it in this imaginary quantitative form to show that, until a large proportion of direct means are used, no direct result may be attained.

We therefore reach the conclusion that, though so-called direct methods are always combinations of direct and indirect means, they are only entitled to the name if the direct means greatly preponderate.

This is as far as a deductive attempt to reach a definition can carry us: the nature of the means and the degree of the preponderance which entitle a method to be called direct can only be determined from usage.

Possibility of a "Direct Method, Limited."

In the teaching of modern languages, no practical difficulty has ever been found in such determination from usage. Throughout the whole course the modern language teacher is improving the pupils' power to think in the language. He has no reasonable motive, after all the labour of the early stages have established the habit, for not letting it develop, as it easily will, in the later stages. The classical teacher may, however, take another view. He may hold that he teaches Latin more quickly and surely by teaching his pupils to think in Latin at the beginning and up to a certain point[1]. He may then urge that, when once the pupils can on demand throw themselves into the Latin set of mind, the facility which they have already acquired can be maintained with less time than would be required to increase it. It is obvious, for instance, that if an hour's Latin were divided, first in such a way that for half-an-hour the lesson were wholly conducted in Latin and for the next half-hour were wholly conducted in English, and secondly in such a way that Latin and English were interspersed throughout, the second method would probably tend to diminish the facility of thinking in Latin while the former would not have that effect. Further, the amount of time given to a modern language is frequently diminished, as the pupils progress, from eight periods a week to as little as three, and progress in thinking in the language still continues. It is difficult to contend that a classical specialist who continues to spend eight periods or even more would lose his facility for thinking in Latin—unless, indeed, he spent less time in direct Latin methods than his schoolfellow spends in direct French methods.

Hence it is for the classical teacher to consider, from the point of view of his aims, such possibilities as the alternation of "free" composition with translation of English into Latin, reading in Latin and translation, a double reading of a passage of an author, conducted in Latin as far as the thought is concerned, and in English as regards the more scientific points of textual and grammatical criticism. For our part, we should distinguish

[1] The preceding paragraphs will have shown the uselessness of beginning with the indirect method and then reverting to the direct. We confine ourselves therefore to the possibility of beginning on direct lines, but later on diluting them.

such alternation of direct and indirect teaching from an attempt to "combine" the two.

CONTENT OF A DIRECT METHOD ACCORDING TO COMMON USAGE.

For establishing what is meant by the direct method in common usage, it might be thought expedient to quote some official or semi-official document. Such may be found in the official French Syllabus of 1902, translated in the Board of Education's Special Reports, Volume XXIV, pp. 46–54. It is, however, too long to reprint; and a briefer and more satisfactory summary is contained in the article by Miss Mary Brebner in Volume III, p. 483. Her summary is as follows:

1. Purely oral teaching at the beginning.
2. The use of the foreign tongue, as much as possible, from the first and throughout.
3. The absolute or partial exclusion of translation from the native into the foreign tongue, except in the higher classes.
4. The reduction to a minimum of translation from the foreign tongue into the mother tongue.
5. The extensive use of pictures in the younger classes, and generally as concrete a way of putting things as possible.
6. The extensive teaching of Realien, i.e. the life, customs and institutions, geography, history and literature of the foreign nation.
7. Constant conversations on the reading-book, either in the form of preparation, or, more frequently, by way of revisal.
8. The use of the reading-book as material for learning grammar inductively.

Of these eight points, we think it will be accepted that all save the sixth are means intended to conduce and in fact are conducive to the end that the pupil shall think in the language which he is studying. The sixth point, though it be adopted by all exponents of the direct method, cannot therefore be considered as more than, in logical language, an "invariable accident," but it is an accident which the classical teacher is not likely to wish to vary. The phraseology of the third and fourth is such as to show that some modern linguists, at least, make some use of alternation of indirect methods. It might be well if these points were re-written in a positive form:

"3. Original composition, oral and written, in the foreign language, without previous thought of the form of expression in the native language.

"4. Training in reading authors for their meaning in the original without translation in word or thought into the native language."

It will then be seen that 1, 2, 5, and 8 substantially concern the earlier stages, and 3, 4, and 7 also embrace the later stages. We should therefore hold that a method as a whole is entitled by common usage to be called direct if (1) it adopts 1, 2, 5, and 8 as its overwhelmingly preponderating method of teaching in the lower stages, and (2) adopts 3 and 4 in their re-written form and 7 as a substantial part of the work at later stages, and uses them in an undiluted form during the period when they are in use, even though other periods of indirect study are alternated in the sense already explained.

Grammar.

It is also important to add that the exponents of the direct method lay no less stress on the need of systematic teaching of accidence and definite teaching of syntax than upholders of the older methods. "Far from being neglected," says the French Syllabus, "the grammar must be taught in an extremely methodical way....But it is chiefly through example that the grammar must be learned." It insists equally strongly that the teacher must plan out the exact vocabulary and exact phrases, as well as the exact constructions and exact forms of accidence which each lesson is to teach, and that each new acquisition should be practised, formulated, revised, and constantly re-practised. No one who has seen the direct method in operation has the smallest doubt that it is a perfectly systematic method. It does not overlook the fact that the learner is perfectly conscious that he is learning and is deliberately setting himself to learn in a way in which the small child learning his own language is not. It does not delude itself with the belief that the pupil will from the first get all his grammatical forms right by the use of unconscious analogy. Doubtless he far sooner is able to reach the right form without conscious thought; this is an undoubted claim put forward by the adherents of the method. The period of conscious thought is only shortened, not eliminated; and it does not involve thought in the mother-tongue.

Plan of Work according to the Direct Method.

The direct method rests on the following principle:

"The essential condition for acquiring a real command of a language—both of the spoken and of the written idiom—is to establish in connection with that language the same habit of direct expression of experience as exists in the use of the mother-tongue, and thereby to develop the power of 'thinking in the foreign language.'

"Since the best means of establishing this Direct Association is the constant hearing and speaking of the language, especially the rapid give-and-take of dialogue, the spoken idiom must be made the basis and, as far as possible, the medium of instruction.

"Further, now that psychological research has shown the important part played in the acquisition of language by auditory impressions and motor activities or reactions (i.e. the cumulative physical experience of hearing and articulation), it is obvious that language teachers must make full use of these factors in the building up of the foreign language in their pupils, instead of relying mainly on the visual experience of the written or printed word.

"This means shifting the centre of gravity of language teaching from the aim of training one's pupils to *understand* the language and *know* its grammar, to the aim of giving one's pupils first and foremost the *command of the language as a means of self-expression*, to serve as a basis for the study of its literature and structure. It means that, especially in the elementary and intermediate stages, the inevitable gap between the 'active' and 'passive' knowledge of the language (i.e. between the power to use it and the power to understand it) should be kept as narrow as possible. In short, the keynote, the guiding principle of the Language Course, must be *self-expression*, with all the forms of intellectual training that this word implies—Composition in its widest sense, both oral and written."

It follows from the considerations here laid down that the intrusion of the mother-tongue into the language class-room must be rigorously restricted, if not deliberately avoided, at every point.

Now, in the acquisition of a language one may distinguish four different processes. They consist in the "understanding" followed by the "use" of new material, i.e. the processes of (i) *interpretation* and (ii) *assimilation*; and in the "understanding" and "use" of old material, i.e. the processes of (iii) *recognition* and (iv) *self-expression* (in all its varying degrees, extending from free reproduction to free composition). In the case of each fresh linguistic acquisition these processes occur in the above order, the last two of course being interchangeable[1]; in practice, however, in any given piece of oral linguistic work the four alternate all the time, but in different proportions, so that it is quite legitimate to say that each of these processes in turn occurs predominantly in one of the following stages of class work: (i) in the reading of a new portion of text used as a basis for definite instruction, (ii) in the reproduction exercises based on that passage, (iii) in the revision of that text or the reading of a similar

[1] That is, the form in which old material (viz., material once assimilated) first reappears may be either as an impression on ear or eye (*recognition*), or as an idea stimulating articulation (*self-expression*).

one, and (iv) in the various exercises in composition in which the knowledge acquired may be turned to account.

Now, whereas translational methods tend to prevent the direct association from being established, by making the mother-tongue intervene in each of these processes or stages, the direct method enables one, in each of them, to dispense with the mother-tongue more and more as the pupils advance, for it is based on a system of reproduction (leading to free composition), in which question and answer in the foreign tongue form the regular means of communication between teacher and taught, the new being linked to and explained by the old at every point, and thus follows a course similar to that of the acquisition and study of the mother-tongue.

It is obvious that the process in which it is most difficult to avoid the intrusion of the mother-tongue is that of *Interpretation*.

Most teachers agree that it is inadvisable to make a fetish of explaining everything in the foreign tongue; but, while some aim deliberately at eventually eliminating the mother-tongue completely from this process, others make a point of using it freely and of testing comprehension by careful translation.

But the essential points, and those on which the exponents of the direct method are in practical agreement, are that

(*a*) Whatever be the treatment applied in the *Interpretation* stage, the stage of *Assimilation* should not be disturbed by the intrusion of the mother-tongue.

(*b*) The old continuous *Construe* should be abandoned altogether, as leading to the reading off of a foreign text in English, and in English of very poor quality indeed.

(*c*) There must be ample opportunity for all the different degrees of self-expression, ranging from free reproduction to free composition.

This implies two kinds of reading—*Intensive* and *Extensive*. On the one hand, the very thorough study of special passages or texts, carefully graduated and selected for the supply of the linguistic and grammatical facts required, these being assimilated by the various processes of reproduction; the aim being that in this portion of the work *everything* should pass into the pupil's "active" control. On the other hand, the reading of complete texts, well within the comprehension of the pupils, so that they can be read rapidly, thus giving that sense of power which is the best incentive to further efforts—texts selected (as early as possible in the language course) for their literary value and for their content, which is summed up at intervals in the form of *précis*, by means of question and answer.

It also implies a continuous and carefully graduated course of composition or self-expression, closely correlated to the reading course, and, indeed, in the lower stages, indistinguishable from it, in which written work is based on oral work and where the passage from reproduction to free composition will occur at every stage of knowledge, free composition constituting the crowning assurance of progress at every step forward.

But it follows from all that has been said that this course of training in self-expression must not be disturbed, above all in its earlier stages, by the regular practice of translation from the mother-tongue into the foreign language, and that this should not be attempted until a considerable mastery of the foreign idiom has been acquired.

There is much difference of opinion as to the proper moment for introducing this form of exercise. It is, however, fairly obvious that, while training in self-expression is an excellent preparation for translation into the foreign tongue, the practice of the latter is by no means the natural approach to self-expression.

Translation *from* the foreign language, accurate and idiomatic translation, stands on quite a different footing, and, provided it is not done often enough to interfere with the direct association and is always limited to short specially selected passages, so that it can be done with the greatest care possible, it supplies a very useful training in accuracy and a convenient test of the understanding of the language, but only one among many. Its use as an exercise in English concerns the language teacher and must be acknowledged, but it is not its "*raison d'être*" and the amount that should be done depends on the number of foreign languages studied by the pupil.

In the higher stages of study the *intensive* as well as the *extensive* reading is supplied by original texts of literary value and the two processes are often combined in the same work. But the principle is still maintained of only devoting part of the pupils' reading to a very thorough and formal study of the text, which always includes the treatment known as "*Lecture Expliquée*" and occasionally culminates in artistic and scholarly translation, whereas other works or portions of the work are read more rapidly for the sake of the content, which is so chosen as to increase the pupils' knowledge and appreciation of the foreign people, its history, and its literature.

To sum up, the new conception of language study is based on the "stylistic" rather than on the grammatical aspect of language. It demands the systematic study of the resources of a language as a means of expression, and not of its structure, except in so far as this is necessary for grammatical correctness.

R. L. ARCHER,
L. C. VON GLEHN.

In 1912 the writer published an appeal[1] to classical teachers in which he urged them to give the direct method a fair trial. A part of it is reprinted here, partly to show how during the last three years the writer's adherence to the direct method has become stricter, and partly because of the interesting *questionnaire* it contains. *A* and *B* were at school when they wrote their experiences; they are now at Cambridge and Oxford respectively, and a few

[1] *Classics and the Direct Method* (Heffer, Cambridge).

changes in the text have accordingly been made. *B*'s answers are remarkably acute, but they show that the "half-direct" method on which he learnt his early work failed to make him fully conscious of a foreign atmosphere —a striking corroboration of the view expressed by Professor Archer in the preceding *Report*.

Everybody will probably agree that the object of education is to develop all the powers of a child, to give him purposes in life, and so to discipline his desires and will that he may always remember that it is as a member of society he must seek his own final good. To accomplish this aim we bring the inherited capacities of the child into contact with a series of environments. We try to make him apprehend some of the most important laws of inanimate and animate nature, and we encourage him to act in accordance with those laws. We try moreover to show him that our own country is not the only one in the world, that foreign nations have something to tell us, and so we teach him at least one foreign language. In order to accomplish our aim more effectually, we teach French or German on the "direct" method; that is, every possible means is employed to introduce into the class-room a French or German environment, and the child is brought as closely as may be into contact with it. He is encouraged to speak, to think and to act, as a young Frenchman or German, so as unconsciously to acquire a sympathetic appreciation of foreigners.

The reformer of classical teaching tries to fit his subject into this general scheme. Those who have the time and ability, he urges, shall be taught something of the virtues of ancient life by thinking, speaking and acting as a Roman or Greek. It is, of course, admitted that only an approximation to this ideal is possible. Even the modern-language teacher, with living civilisations around him, is but partially successful, and endeavours to send his pupils abroad for a short period. Any revival of a classical environment is necessarily far more unsatisfactory and imperfect, and makes serious claims upon the skill of the teacher. But this very drawback turns out to be really, in some respects at least, a positive gain. The constant effort, on the part of both teacher and taught, to reconstruct ancient life is a valuable training and discipline of the imagination. And it is in proportion to our powers of reviving this old-world life that we can learn the lessons a study of classical antiquity ought to inculcate—citizenship, discipline, piety, love of beauty and devotion to truth.

This general principle commits the reformer to certain subordinate principles of instruction.

(1) The method of teaching must be that called "direct"; that is, the foreign language must be associated as far as possible directly with things, ideas and feelings, without the intervention of the mother tongue.

(2) The lessons of ancient life are embodied in literature, and that literature cannot be thoroughly appreciated by anybody unless he can speak, and apprehend when spoken, the ancient languages. Two *tongues*, in fact, are among the most valuable heirlooms of antiquity.

(3) Every effort must be made to realise the melody of these tongues by scrupulous attention to pronunciation, accent and quantity.

(4) The stages of teaching preparatory to a systematic study of the surviving literature must be rendered instructive by the use of pictures, of easy stories of ancient life told and reproduced in Latin and Greek, and by the acting of simple plays, specially written for this purpose, which illustrate ancient life and thought. No means must be neglected of making the pupil live again, as far as this is possible, the lives of Roman and Greek children. He must hear, speak and read their language, and act scenes which might have taken place two thousand years ago.

The method actually adopted is, with certain unimportant variations of detail, roughly as follows:

(1) The pupil comes to school with a knowledge of

English obviously acquired on the "direct" method. This knowledge is made the basis of a thorough course of instruction in pure grammar, to be used as a help in the study of any foreign language.

(2) He is carefully trained in practical phonetics.

(3) The first lessons in a foreign language deal with the simple actions of everyday life, which the pupil performs and describes (in Latin and Greek) under the guidance of the teacher. The foreign grammar is learned after this drill, and, as far as possible, in the foreign language. The training in pure grammar makes this comparatively easy. No work is committed to writing before it has been thoroughly understood in oral practice.

(4) Then comes the stage of stories and acting. After drill in the fresh grammatical points, a story is told and explained by the teacher in the foreign language. The pupils repeat it, and are questioned by the teacher to see if everything is understood. It is then written out. Plays are acted on a similar method, the pupils taking different parts in turn. Pictures also are employed at this stage, descriptions of them being worked out by the teacher and pupils in collaboration. Oral practice again precedes writing.

(5) In the next stage classical authors are studied, at first the simplest texts. These are read aloud, explained in Latin or Greek, and summarised by the pupils in the foreign language. Considerable portions are reproduced in the form of "free" composition, or learnt by heart as home-work. Stories are told and reproduced as in the preceding stage.

(6) Up to this point English is avoided as much as possible, being used only when the teacher cannot make himself understood without it. Translation, too, both to and from English, is reduced to a minimum, and is used only for the purpose of testing knowledge already acquired. But by the time the pupil reaches the upper fifth and sixth forms, he begins to translate as an exercise in a difficult literary art. Attention is paid to style and diction, and nonsense is never tolerated. Authors are

read, as before; free composition and translation from English are regularly practised, and great care is bestowed upon a systematic revision of grammar. Verses are begun at this stage, and translation into English verse is occasionally attempted. Those who have specialised in classics are now prepared for the University scholarship examinations. The pupils who specialise in other subjects leave off classics (or Latin, if they have not begun Greek) at an early period in this stage.

It must not be supposed that all reformers adhere rigidly to the above methods, although most are agreed upon the principles which underlie them. The present writer does not believe that the course outlined is ideal, but he has tried to describe the methods which teachers are tending to adopt. In order to satisfy his own mind he has submitted a series of questions to two students, hereafter styled *A* and *B*. Both of them have learnt French and German entirely on the direct method. *A* obtained a first class in the tripos of 1915; *B* is a scholar of Balliol. It is worth recording that the following questions were submitted to *A* and *B* independently, and were answered, after careful deliberation, in writing. Of course these boys are not infallible judges, but their evidence is at least thoughtful and sincere.

Though *A* and *B* differ, this difference is not that between a supporter and an opponent of reform; the critical attitude of *B* is due to the nature of the questions, which were chosen with a view to eliciting any limitations to the rigid application of the direct method to Latin. Hence *B*'s answers lay stress upon what appear to be necessary violations of that method, but really his evidence is all in support of its main principles.

Question 1. Assuming a good knowledge of "pure" or "universal" grammar, do you think that you could have readily learnt to understand and write Latin without the use of English? If you wish to qualify your answer, state clearly the exceptions you make.

Answer of A

I think Latin could be understood — even appreciated — and

Answer of B

I do not think a knowledge of pure grammar would have

written, though at *some* sacrifice of completeness and accuracy. But it is not necessary for knowledge to be complete at first, provided that it grows in accuracy and fulness, as it does under the direct method.

made much difference. It would have made it possible to learn the preliminary grammar more rapidly and with less English, but the elements of grammar are soon "picked up." In any case some English would be necessary; e.g. in dealing with the uses of the Latin dative and ablative. In the initial stage everything seems very hazy and muddled, and for a really clear explanation of these cases, or other complicated points, English must be used. Time itself, however, helps to correct this vagueness.

Question 2. Are you conscious of a Roman "atmosphere" during your Latin lessons?

Answer of A

Pictures, models, etc., and descriptions furnished by the teacher certainly supply the "physical" parts of the "atmosphere." Progress in reading gradually fills in the rest of this and the intellectual side as well.

Answer of B

If a Roman atmosphere means feeling and thinking from a Roman point of view, very little. What I read I think about and criticise in English, and very much from a present-day standpoint.

Question 3. Were you conscious of a Roman "atmosphere" during your first Latin lessons?

Answer of A

I think I was first conscious of it when I knew enough Latin to appreciate picture stories, or to read, as a complete whole, short descriptive stories.

Answer of B

No: the attention was too much taken up with details (grammar, words, etc.).

Question 4. Would you have been more conscious of such an atmosphere if your early lessons had been conducted more consistently on the direct method?

Answer of A

Very probably, provided that the teacher had exercised the greatest care (even ingenuity) in building up a suitable vocabulary by such processes of demonstra-

Answer of B

I think not. I was very grateful for a little English, occasionally, to clear up difficulties. Anyway, such an atmosphere seems impossible before

tion as might have been unmistakable to all. A beginner in any language is very apt to form wrong, and lasting, impressions, unless corrected.

some idea is acquired of Rome and the Romans.

Question 5. Are you conscious of a Greek "atmosphere" during your Greek lessons?

Answer of A

One comes to feel a Greek "atmosphere" just in the same way as a Roman atmosphere.

Answer of B

Same as No. 2. The "atmosphere" is really generated by the master himself.

Question 6. Did your knowledge of Latin enable you to master Greek more easily on the direct method?

Answer of A

Certainly; the declensions and grammar of Latin prepared me for the very similar declensions, etc., of Greek.

Answer of B

The knowledge of Latin made Greek far easier, and helped the direct method very much, so that progress was rapid.

Question 7. Do you now associate Latin with things and ideas, or do English words force themselves upon the consciousness?

Answer of A

In ordinary conversation one can almost always find readily Latin turns of expression. Only in cases of somewhat exceptional difficulty does the mind call up an English word or phrase for want of a Latin one.

Answer of B

With special names of trees, fishes, etc., I think of the English. If I see a solitary word, e.g. "res," "do," I mechanically think of "thing," "give"; but if I see a phrase, "tota res perdita est," or "vasta dabo," I at once feel what the Latin means without thinking of any English. When reading Latin I usually understand at once, but I should hesitate if asked to translate.

Question 8. Do you find that an explanation in English of a word or construction interrupts the current of your thoughts, or destroys the Roman "atmosphere," during your present Latin lessons? Is an entirely Latin lesson more enjoyable than one containing translation?

Answer of A

I do not find such pieces of English thrown in quite appro-

Answer of B

I never feel any serious break, as even in a Latin lesson

priate. A really vigorous lesson completely in Latin would, I think, be more *enjoyable*.

But there is the *practical* side. For this I consider some English necessary *somewhere*. Could not the teacher have something in the way of an informal "question-time," when each pupil should get his own difficulties explained? This would, of course, be apart, and time would be allowed between the reading and the asking of the questions for the pupil to think over his difficulties, and, if possible, to solve them for himself. In any case he might like a confirmation of his views, or the reverse if he is wrong.

I think for the most part in English, at any rate whenever I think *carefully* about anything. I do a certain amount of English thinking even in French and German lessons conducted entirely in those languages.

An entirely Latin lesson is usually more enjoyable, because I can simply enjoy the Latin without having to think of an English *translation*.

Question 9. Do you think that your progress in Latin would be retarded by the entire omission of English?

Answer of A

I think the progress would not be so *sure*, even though it might be *swifter*. English *tests* knowledge already gained.

Answer of B

Yes. (1) A difficult point can seldom be satisfactorily thrashed out in Latin. (2) Literary discussions or remarks, explanations of points of philosophy, etc., are best in English. (3) Some passages need translation; e.g. Virgil's lines about the Labyrinth gave us a distinct impression, but it was not until we tried to translate and analyse them that we saw how little we had mastered them.

Question 10. Do you find an English "construe" a real help? If so, would you prefer to have a Latin explanation of difficulties first?

Answer of A

"Construes" are of help sometimes to explain difficulties. I should certainly prefer a Latin explanation beforehand.

Answer of B

I have never done an English "construe" in class, but I think that, when the difficult points have been explained, a "construe" would be waste of time. A literal translation I think useful (1) as a help when working alone; (2) in school work, when going over what I have already done, to see if I have not missed any points or unconsciously misunderstood some passage (which often happens).

Question 11. Do you consider it helpful to make a translation for yourself?

Answer of A

To make a translation, e.g. of Thucydides' speeches, I consider most beneficial. To make a translation, e.g. of his narrative parts, I consider a nuisance and a waste of time.

Answer of B

It always shows up points that have been missed, and prevents forgetting, but it takes too much time.

Question 12. Do you consider it helpful to have a good translation read to you after the discussion of a passage?

Answer of A

I consider this most useful *after doing one for myself*. But in any case it would probably be of some use, though perhaps a translation given by the teacher, with remarks on style, might be better. The teacher knows what style best suits his pupils.

Answer of B

More of a pleasure than a help. The discussion should have finished with difficulties; and if it is desired, after details have been dealt with, to get a proportioned view of the whole passage, I prefer to re-read it in the original.

Question 13. When writing "free" composition do you ever find yourself unconsciously translating from English?

Answer of A

The preliminary outline is almost bound to shape itself in English thought. Then one thinks of appropriate Latin words, etc., and, once getting on the way, one proceeds for the most part in the spirit of the Latin alone — without translating.

Answer of B

Very seldom. Usually a rough sketch of what I am going to say comes into my mind in English, but when I write I do not think of English as a rule, and find it difficult to give an English translation of what I have written.

Question 14. Is free composition a useful preparation for translation from English?

Answer of A

Free composition teaches idiom, order of words, etc.

Answer of B

Very useful indeed, because it gives you the habit of writing Latin and Greek idiom instead of English, so that, when it comes to translation from English, you do not try to do it literally.

Question 15. Can you think in Latin and in Greek?

Answer of A

Prompt and unhesitating response in conversation in Greek and Latin (such as one attains to under the direct method) on simple topics implies *unconscious* thinking in Latin and Greek.

Answer of B

Only about simpler things. Thus when I write free composition I usually think in the language, because there the style is more important than the matter.

But over some difficulty in reading, or anything serious, I think in English.

Latin and Greek of *ordinary* difficulty I always understand without translating or needing a translation. I prefer not to have an English version if I can do without it.

Question 16. Does translation either into or from English confirm the knowledge you have already acquired?

Answer of A

I should prefer the use of Latin phrases for manipulation (instead of English for translation) to give practice in constructions already learnt. The pupil should be told what constructions he must use in a piece of free composition.

Answer of B

Translation into English always makes you sure of a passage, and translation from English is still more important. Thus you may know some phrase you have met in your reading, but it is seldom that you make it your own, and have it ready, until you have used it to express some corresponding English idiom. In free composition you may use only the constructions you are familiar with, unless special directions are given.

Question 17. Have you any decided opinion as to the value of the direct method compared with that of the old?

Answer of A

I think the great superiority of the direct over the indirect method lies in the intellectual activity which it necessitates as opposed to the other system where a bare equivalent of some Latin or Greek word is thrown at the pupil—for him to forget, just because his *mind* has never acted on the word. Surely "ideas" or "things" (the instruments of the direct method) are to be preferred to mere "words" and "equivalents."

Answer of B

Its chief value is:
- (i) That it makes the lesson far more interesting;
- (ii) That it teaches literary appreciation, and makes it possible after a comparatively short time to read purely for pleasure.

Its chief disadvantages are:
- (i) That so much depends on the teacher and his personality;
- (ii) That it gives (unless great care be taken) a tendency to inaccuracy in details which is difficult to conquer.

These answers suggest certain reflexions. All minds are not alike; some work best along certain lines, others work best along other lines. Though both heartily support the direct method, *B* feels the need of English (for *explanations*, not as translation) far more than *A*. This may not be due to the partial application of the direct method in their early lessons, since both have gone through the same course of training, and been subjected to exactly the same influences. Nor can the mind of the pupil be entirely freed from the habits of thought unconsciously formed by the continual use of the mother-tongue in ordinary intercourse. *B* is conscious of thinking in English even during the French lessons, where the direct method has far greater scope than in the Latin class. As both *A* and *B* feel the need of some English for the explanation of special difficulties, the master must not make a fetish of "all Latin," and he would do well to remember that some pupils need more English than others. But, such is human infirmity, the more English he gives them, the more they will want. The use of English is, in the earlier stages at least, a kind of drug habit.

Both *A* and *B* are conscious that the direct method is better and more stimulating than the old. Translation they find useful, but only because it tests, corrects or confirms knowledge already acquired. No one can translate until he fully comprehends the meaning of the original, and both *A* and *B* agree in holding that the explanation of the original should be, as far as possible, in that language. *A* thinks that there is no reason why all lessons should not be almost entirely in Latin, except for the demands made upon the teacher's skill. See his answer to (4).

It is clear that a danger lies in dealing with single words rather than with phrases or sentences. A single word like "res" tends to summon to the foreground of consciousness a single English equivalent, and it is well known that very few English words exactly correspond to Latin or Greek words. The master, therefore, should try to build up round e.g. "res" a mass of associations by means of phrases and sentences in which that word is appropriately used. The best way is to note the context of "res" when it occurs in the reader.

A Roman or a Greek atmosphere is only formed by slow degrees. Here the teacher's appliances, skill and enthusiasm are of supreme importance. As *B* says, it is the master who "generates the atmosphere." Hence the necessity of models, restorations, pictures, "picture-stories," simple readers and plays. All these are wanted in great numbers, so that criticism and experience may select the most useful. A preparatory course of lessons on ancient history, topography and so on, would be an invaluable introduction to Latin and Greek.

But it may well be urged that, even though the reformed methods produce good scholars, they are not necessarily more efficient than the old. To such an objection it can be replied that oral methods are more rapid than the old, and save time. Further, they are more effective, because they train the ear and the vocal organs as well as the eye, affecting the brain through three avenues instead of through one. But the most telling answer is given by an examination of the results. It is certain that any University teacher would prefer to have *A* and *B* as pupils rather than students of equal ability trained in the ordinary manner. They are keener, brighter and more alive than most young men of similar age and attainments. They are interested in intellectual things generally, and are never bored or "stale." It is a common cry nowadays that a classical training unfits a man for life, dulling, instead of sharpening, his faculties. The charge is a true one, in so far as our present classical education often deals with words and verbal equivalents, being far removed from life and reality. But such an objection cannot be fairly brought against the training advocated by the reformers. Besides *A* and *B*, the present writer knows about twelve classical men who have been educated on reformed lines for the greater part of their career. One has three first classes in triposes to his credit, another two, four others one. Two have gained Fellowships. They are all intelligent and efficient workers, able and willing to serve their day and generation. Their interests are by no means confined to classics. One, indeed, is a classical schoolmaster and an enthusiastic reformer; others have found their vocation in careers in which a classical training is of no direct service. Most of them are good actors, and all of them are agreeable companions, and able to deal with men as well as with things. They have none of the faults usually laid to the charge of classical men. It may also be mentioned that there are at the Universities five or six others, holding good scholarships, and promising to be equally efficient.

Finally, reformers find that even those who study the classics only for a few years learn how to read Latin and Greek with pleasure and profit, a result rarely achieved by the old system.

The present writer would like to close his short account with an appeal to classical teachers, both those in schools and those at the Universities. Some of them have in the past seen classics being taught on reformed methods, and have perhaps gone away dissatisfied. Will they think twice before condemning the principles of the reformers? May not the fault lie with details of method, or with the imperfect skill of the teacher? The reform is in its infancy; mistakes have been made, and many points remain to be worked out. But progress is rapid, and during the last few years an enormous improvement has taken place, as anybody will admit who attended the Summer Schools of Latin at Bangor and Cambridge. Perhaps the greatest obstacle to progress is the character of our elementary examinations. These are not adapted to the attainments of young pupils taught with other aims in view than the power to translate and to answer questions on grammatical details. That the final results are satisfactory can no longer be denied, but the steps leading to the end are by no means the steps of the older methods. Is it chimerical to hope that examiners will acknowledge the new forces at work, and sometimes offer alternative questions?

Reformers plead for a fair hearing. They have unshaken faith in their principles. They believe in the value of a classical education, if conducted on right lines; and they know that classics will die, both in schools and in Universities, unless the old methods and principles are abandoned. But they are aware that perfection is not attained at once. They wish to improve and systematise their methods, and heartily welcome sympathetic criticism. But their critics ought not to condemn the principles because the methods are not faultless, or because they are unacquainted with the progress made during the last few years. Above all, let them remember that the reformers are but human, and therefore liable to err. There have been failures—though not many—among the reformers' pupils. Is it fair to lay the blame upon the new ideal of a classical education? May not the cause be the imperfection of a teacher feeling his way to higher things? The present writer, at any rate, admits, with regret and shame, his own share in retarding what he is convinced is a sensible and healthy reform.

CHAPTER II

THE IDEAL BEGINNER

Complete success with the direct method can be obtained only if the learner be carefully prepared during early boyhood. From the age of about nine he should be taken through a course of study to facilitate the mastery of foreign languages. This course, as will be seen, helps a learner to acquire any language, and not merely Latin and Greek. Indeed it is a great pity that language teachers work in water-tight compartments without any serious effort at correlation[1]. Only when language-training is treated as a unity, with a definite common aim, and with systematic co-ordination of methods, can the best results be achieved. This unity is not artificial, but living and natural. The languages that a boy learns at school have a very large common element. In all of them we find the division of a sentence into subject and predicate, parts of speech with practically the same functions, and words grouped into phrases, clauses and sentences, the last of which may be either simple or complex. In all also the fundamental principles of literary composition are almost identical; every piece of artistic work must be an organised whole, with beginning, middle and end. Clearness, precision and force are always literary virtues and their opposites literary faults. The sounds, too, although not always represented by the same letters or combinations of letters, are to a

[1] The recent attempt to adopt a uniform grammatical terminology has ended in failure.

great extent common to Greek, Latin, German, French, and, in a less degree, English.

These common essentials should be carefully studied before any foreign language is attempted, but because it is nobody's business to teach them they are very rarely taught. Nothing elaborate is desired or necessary; half an hour each day for a year or, at the most, two years, would produce the desired result by the time the pupil reaches the age of eleven. Obviously the instruction can only be given in English, and it has always seemed to the writer that the English masters are the right and proper persons to give it. The reply generally given is: "We do not need this knowledge for English teaching; if you want it for Latin, teach it yourself." This retort not only begs a very important question, but assumes that each language is shut off from all others, while the common aim of all literary training is ignored. But, whoever be the teacher, the beginner in Latin ought to have received a training in phonetics, general grammar and the main principles of simple composition. He should also have learnt French for at least one year.

The training in phonetics should be strictly practical, and deal mainly with the vowel sounds. These in English are chiefly diphthongal, pure vowels being comparatively rare. Young boys quickly learn how to produce these sounds, while considerable difficulty is often experienced by older boys when the vocal organs have grown stiff and fixed habits of speech have been formed. Let it be clearly understood that nothing elaborate is required. The essential thing is to acquire the power to distinguish the vowel sounds and to practise the proper way of producing them. After this training no difficulty is experienced in pronouncing Latin clearly and with accuracy. The "reformed" pronunciation should be adopted, not only because it is, approximately at least, the pronunciation of the Ciceronian age, but also because in it one sound only corresponds to one letter or to one group of letters. Now oral work forms a large part of teaching on the direct method, and for successful oral work such a pronunciation, at least in the earlier stages, is absolutely necessary. When the master pronounces a word its spelling must be at once obvious to every member of the class. It is therefore necessary that the sound should have one, and only one, written representation. Fortunately the reformed pronunciation is of this character, but, as Professor Postgate points out[1], if a boy has "*incipit insipiens*" read out to him with the English pronunciation, how is he to take it down? It would be a great boon if the reformed pronunciation were adopted throughout the country. We should then have uniformity, instead of the confusion which often upsets a boy's work for a term or more after a migration from one school to another. The training of the vocal organs, if careful and thorough, is a great gain intellectually. Clear speaking helps, indeed produces, clear thinking[2].

The second requisite in our ideal beginner is a knowledge of general grammar. It is ignorance of this which, more than anything else, has retarded classical studies for the last twenty years, not only in this country but also in France[3]. In Germany the need is fully recognised[4],

[1] *How to Pronounce Latin*, p. 12.

[2] Sir Clifford Allbutt in *Proceedings of the Classical Association*, 1906, pp. 19 ff.

[3] See on this subject the excellent book of J. Bezard, *Comment apprendre le Latin à nos fils*, especially pp. 1–30.

[4] See the Board of Education Special Report 20, *The Teaching of Classics in Secondary Schools in Germany*, pp. 58, 64, 65, 132–137.

but in Britain a state of hopeless muddle has existed ever since the revolt—a perfectly justified revolt—against excessive parsing and analysis. Again let it be clearly understood that elaborate detail is neither asked for nor necessary. A clear knowledge of the various types of sentence, of the essential parts of a sentence, and of the rules of concord, is quite sufficient. But although little is required, that little must be thoroughly mastered. Hazy notions are worse than useless. The pupil should be able to say what part of speech any word is in a given context, to pick out the subject, direct object, and so on, of any straightforward sentence, and to detect ordinary grammatical blunders. It is sheer nonsense to maintain, as many do, that knowledge of this sort is useless. On the contrary, it is of inestimable value for all language-teaching, besides conducing to lucidity of thought and logical precision.

The writer is not asking for new subjects to be added to the curriculum; he is merely urging that a change be made in the scope of two subjects often, if not always, included in it. Most schools teach practical phonetics as a propaedeutic to French, and English grammar as a part of the English course. But there is not enough co-ordination of this work with the learning of other languages, and the object in view is far too narrow. Phonetics and general grammar are common to all linguistic studies, and should be treated as such. The ground covered should be limited, and the treatment severely practical, but within the limits fixed everything should be so thoroughly learnt as to form part of the pupil's mental stock-in-trade.

The ideal beginner needs to be familiar with the main principles of literary composition. Skill in this is easily acquired if general grammar be carefully taught. But as it is, beginners in Latin often have no clear ideas of sentence-structure, and write English sentences which are ungrammatical, ambiguous and innocent of punctuation. How can a foreign language be successfully attempted under such conditions? Surely recent efforts to improve the subject matter of a boy's essays, to adapt it to the content of the young mind, should not blind us to the value of the formal side of composition. Language must submit to the discipline of rules unless we are going to be content with a garden of weeds. Only the genius can speak and write clearly and forcibly without the aid of discipline in form, and geniuses are few and far between. It is strongly urged that before a pupil attempts any foreign language he should be impressed with the truth that each sentence he writes must conform to certain rules, some of them peculiar to the new language and some common to all languages. The latter should have been understood, thoroughly learnt and constantly practised, in the medium of the mother tongue. It is to persistent drill of this kind that the French owe, not only their skill as linguists, but also much of the lucidity and grace of their literature.

It is now generally agreed among teachers that French should be begun at least one year (or by preference two years) before a start is made with a second language. The stupid folly of initiating a child of eight or nine years into French, Latin and Greek at one and the same time is now happily a thing of the past. It is through the medium of French that the pupil first understands what is meant by an inflected language, and learns his first paradigms. Will the French master think it too much for us to ask if we suggest that periodically—say once a term—he might give, in English, a lesson emphasising the difference between an uninflected and an inflected language, taking as his material English on the one hand and, on the other, such French inflexions as have already been learnt by the class? Immediate advantage to the work in French may not result from these lessons, but if thoughtfully given they will arouse a boy's interest and educate his mind to appreciate linguistic differences, and in this way all his subsequent training will benefit. Perhaps the Latin master will be able, later on, to repay his colleague with compound interest.

These initial stages, in fact, demand the heartiest co-operation between the masters concerned. They must realise that they have a common aim, namely, to develop linguistic skill and literary appreciation, and they must subordinate to this all secondary objects. Each master will at the outset state clearly what co-operation his own subject stands in need of, and he will be prepared to comply with his colleagues' requests.

Finally, the beginner ought to feel an interest in the Romans as a people; he should have learnt from his historical study that modern civilisation is based upon Roman, that the Romance languages have grown out of Latin, and that the Latin vocabulary has given us a very large proportion of our English words.

Let us sum up once more our requirements in the ideal beginner.

(1) The power to distinguish and correctly to produce:

(*a*) the pure vowel sounds, open and closed, long and short;

(*b*) the diphthongs;

(*c*) the dentals and gutturals.

(2) A knowledge of "pure" or universal grammar, including:

(*a*) simple analysis of sentences;

(*b*) power to distinguish the various parts of speech;
(*c*) the functions of words, phrases, clauses and sentences.

(3) Skill in writing grammatical and accurately punctuated English sentences.

(4) Some appreciation of the place of Rome in the history of civilisation.

On this foundation a sound superstructure can be built. Without it success will be very uncertain. The first steps are generally decisive of future progress, and if the pupil take a dislike to a subject because of his unprepared state, the educational value of his subsequent training will be altogether lost.

CHAPTER III[1]

TRANSLATION, COMPOSITION, GRAMMAR

§ 1. TRANSLATION.

When a ripe scholar is translating, say from Greek into English, his mind is engaged in certain complex processes of thought. The Greek is examined to discover, first, the general drift of the piece, secondly, the full force of every word in its own context, thirdly, the effect of order, the various degrees of emphasis, and so forth.

[1] It is conventional to call renderings from English "composition," renderings into English "translation." "Direct" teachers, however, tend to call all versions, whether into or from English, "translations," and to limit the term "composition" to exercises of self-expression. Some inconsistency in the use of these words occurs in the following chapters. To be perfectly consistent has been found impossible, but in every case the nature of the context will prevent misconception.

Then the mind turns to English, and tries to discover ways of representing all that the Greek has suggested to it. There is gradually worked out an English version, with the words in an English order, with English sentence-structure, and with emphasis expressed in an English way. The success of a translation depends upon the translator's knowledge of both languages; if either language has been imperfectly mastered, the version will be proportionately inadequate. The actual making of the version does not increase the translator's knowledge of either language; it only increases his familiarity with both, that is, it gives him a chance of using knowledge already acquired, and so of making it readier for future use. It may perhaps be argued that this account is contradicted by experience; that generations of learners have used the method of translation and no other method. This contention is open to doubt. Translating confirms knowledge and drives home what has been already learnt, but it cannot impart the unknown. Fresh information, on the traditional method, is assimilated by the study of rules, and by the comparison of examples with a given translation, such examples being always a marked feature of old-fashioned text-books. Let it be understood that translation has its uses, that it is an exercise of great value, and that it must find a place in any system of language-teaching; but it is equally important to remember that it can impart no new knowledge, although the comparison of original with version may do so to a considerable extent. Indeed, this use of translations has been curiously neglected in the past. It is quite a valuable exercise for a pupil to discover, from a given version, how the English is derived from the original. Fresh knowledge, in short, can be acquired from a *translation*, but not from *translating*.

Under the direct method translating is employed for three quite distinct purposes: (1) as a test, (2) to drive home grammatical rules, (3) as a literary art. It is, of course, during the latter period of the course that literary translation is practised, but right from the very first progress is tested by occasional exercises in turning short sentences (or even phrases and words) from one language into another. For example, the teacher may have been explaining, during one of the very early lessons, the phrase "spectare libros (librum)." This he would proceed to do by repeating, with dramatic action, such sentences as:

librum specto;
tu, Marce, librum non spectas;
spectate libros, discipuli.

But he now wishes to discover whether the phrase is really understood. One way of doing this is to ask a few questions in Latin, such as:

spectone librum meum, Sexte?
quid facit Sextus, Tite?
quis librum non spectat, Marce?

Even though these and similar questions be correctly answered, he may not be quite sure that the dullest boys have mastered the point. Accordingly he asks for a translation of one of the above sentences. The other day the writer was explaining the poem on Lesbia's sparrow to a class of beginners. The last two lines:

tua nunc opera meae puellae
flendo turgiduli rubent ocelli,

lend themselves very well to the method of paraphrase. It was easy to explain "rubere" by pointing to a book of the proper colour and saying: "liber rubet." That "ocelli" means "eyes" was at once understood, but no attempt was made to explain the force of the diminutive. This could easily have been done, but did not occur to the writer at the time. "Tua opera" was the phrase that presented most difficulty. As the class knew that "verbum" and "nomen" mean "verb" and "noun" respectively, the following conversation took place:

Magister. "Opera" est nomen; "animum attendere" est verbum. Intellegitisne "animum attendere"?

Pueri. Intellegimus.

Magister. Puella Catulli flet tua opera, Orce. Flet quia tu, Orce, passerem abstulisti, quia animum ad passerem attendisti. "Opera" fere idem significat quod "cura," "studium."

The class was then asked for a translation of "tua opera," and several boys suggested "all through you," thus showing that they had understood the explanation.

The second use of translation is to confirm knowledge already gained, or partially gained. For example, a series of very easy English sentences, illustrating the difference between the nominative and the accusative, may be set for translation as soon as the constructions of the subject and of the direct object have been used and explained. Every new construction should be treated in this way, due care being taken that the exercises be not too frequent or too monotonous. Some supporters of the direct method would eliminate such exercises altogether for the first two years of Latin, but experience proves that they are useful and necessary. One point may be noticed here which is of great importance in all the work of the earlier part of the course. The sentences should be worked through orally before a written translation is attempted. Mistakes are bound to occur, and these are better corrected orally, for *littera scripta manet.*

Everything that is committed to writing tends to re-appear afterwards, and it is therefore well to insure that as few errors as possible are perpetuated in this way[1]. Later on, when confidence and ease have been obtained, this preliminary oral preparation can be omitted.

Finally, translation may be practised as an art—perhaps the most difficult of all the literary arts. When translation of this kind should be begun will depend mainly upon the amount of time which is devoted to classical work. Roughly speaking, the fifth and sixth forms are those best able to profit by it, but occasionally quite good results are obtained with a fourth form. But, whenever it is begun, a very high ideal of both accuracy and style should be set and consistently maintained.

All translation of the last sort needs a careful study of the original text before it is attempted. Naturally the preparation done by the teacher will grow less as time goes on, until all can be left to the pupil himself. At first, however, the preparation must be thorough, and be conducted by the teacher. It will be entirely in Latin (or Greek) and will consist of paraphrase, explanations of difficulties, and exposition of subject matter. This has as its aim the formation of good habits of translation, which are greatly encouraged when the mind is free to work out a version without being distracted by grammatical difficulties, and when bad tendencies are not fixed as bad habits by the committal to writing of faults and blunders. Not until the master is fairly certain that the passage as

[1] The strong tendency for a writer to repeat words or constructions he has recently used might be illustrated by quotations from many authors. It often leads to faults of style, but if properly regulated it is a source of strength. We learn to use words and constructions, not by discussions about them, but by using them. In this way mainly is our vocabulary increased and flexibility of expression acquired.

a whole and each sentence separately are understood by all will he allow a translation to be made. In time the written version can be done as home-work (or in class) without further aid, but not at first. Boys have to be taught how to translate both by precept and by example; so master and boys together should work out a translation bit by bit. Principles of translation need emphasis and illustration, and every effort should be made to enlarge the vocabulary of English words habitually employed by the class. Accuracy, ease, clearness and vigour are the qualities most to be aimed at, and the master ought to be a ruthless critic until they are secured.

When the pupil can translate easy passages with tolerable accuracy, the time has arrived when he will derive great advantage from a series of lessons dealing methodically with the sentence-structure of English, Latin and Greek, and especially with characteristic differences. Knowledge of this kind cannot be "picked up"; it must be taught, and taught thoroughly. But, so far as the writer's experience goes, very few teachers indeed attempt a systematic treatment of the subject. A word of warning is necessary. This series of lessons must not come too soon; a generalisation is never appreciated until the mind has become acquainted with many particular instances. So, without postponing the course until too late, care must be taken not to make it premature. The second term in the fifth form is suggested as a suitable period, and the time spent should be one lesson each fortnight.

§ 2. UNSEENS.

The practice of unseen translation is not neglected by teachers on the direct method. But it does not form a regular part of the curriculum until the fourth year of Latin and the third year of Greek. The reasons for postponement are two. In the first place, nearly every reading lesson affords the same intellectual exercise as the working out of an unseen. In the second place, translation as an art cannot successfully be attempted until the pupil's mind has reached a fairly high stage of development, and premature efforts are bound to result in the formation of habits of guessing and of slipshod writing.

When the proper time has arrived, the subject is treated carefully and systematically. The master gives one or two demonstration lessons, in which he emphasises the various steps by which a tolerable version is finally obtained. These are roughly four in number.

(1) The passage is read over silently once (or twice), so that the general drift is caught. Unknown words are noted.

(2) An effort is made to work out each sentence, in the light of the general sense, by the aid of grammar and order of words. Parts that defy solution are noted.

(3) Idiomatic English equivalents for portions of each sentence are carefully chosen.

(4) After a last attempt to see whether the context does not clear up the parts still unknown, a complete translation is written out.

Two principles should always be borne in mind. They are:

(1) the translation *must* make good sense; yet

(2) every word, every grammatical fact, *must* be accounted for.

These two principles, consciously or unconsciously applied, are at once the suggestive stimulus and the critical check which result in a correct version. All mistakes and all faults are caused by neglect of one or the other, or of both.

The demonstration lessons include advice as to the limits of legitimate guessing, and insist on the importance of consciousness of ignorance, where ignorance exists, so as to reduce the number of blunders by excluding that hazy state of mind when a boy thinks he knows the meaning of a sentence, but is not sure that he knows. A warning is given against common errors and pitfalls. One of the most treacherous of these lies in translating the relative. An inflected relative, with endings marking number and gender, can refer to a distant antecedent; the English relative, with case-inflexions only, refers to the nearest preceding substantive. Forgetfulness of this may result in nonsense being written, even when the translator has worked out the meaning correctly.

When unseens first become a part of the course they should err on the side of easiness rather than that of difficulty, and it is a very good plan to take them from the same plain text that is being read in class. In this way difficulties of style and subject matter are to some extent avoided. A passage for unseen translation should, whenever possible, be a fairly complete whole, written in an interesting way, and instructive in its content. A dull piece never produces such good results as a bright, attractive one.

There is a very good reason why unseens should not be set too frequently. Careful correction of each version with individual boys is necessary, as questions of style and idiom are of constant occurrence, and time does not permit such individual attention to be given at too frequent intervals. Hasty correction often leads to hasty performance, but every version should, in its way, be a little work of art, and be treated accordingly. In order to secure adequate practice, the writer has adopted with success the plan of oral unseen translation. The same steps are followed as were recommended for written work, and the co-operation of class and master results in a rendering which, to a certain extent, may be taken as a model for unaided efforts.

§ 3. Composition.

Composition in an ancient language is a means and not an end, except in the case of mature scholars, whose efforts afford a considerable amount of aesthetic pleasure. A realisation of this truth has, in recent years, caused composition to be much depreciated, especially Greek composition and Latin verses. In Germany composition has long been relegated to a very subordinate position. "Not a few prominent men are in favour of still further reducing the amount of Latin composition, either confining it practically to retranslation, or abolishing it altogether in the last three years of the Gymnasium, as it has been already abolished in the Realgymnasium. Paulsen goes so far as to say that every hour spent on writing Latin, save in so far as it improves the power of reading, is, to use Mommsen's phrase, 'thrown into the water, if not worse.' We should say that there was nothing like Latin prose to bring a boy face to face with the real thought of an English author, and make him wrestle with the sense, stripping the thought bare of all verbal wrappings and trimmings. Many in Germany will meet this with a direct negative[1]." This depreciation of composition can easily be carried too far. "Thorough" is our watchword, and it may well be doubted whether any language can be thoroughly learnt without constant practice in using it. A language is after all a means of self-expression as well as the key to the understanding of another person's words, and the two functions are so closely connected that the one can never be neglected without endangering the operation of the other[2]. So, whatever the aim of teaching Latin, understanding and self-expression will, from the very first, go on simultaneously. Of course at first the pupil's task will be easy, being in fact almost entirely imitative. But gradually and systematically more is required, until the exercises, whether oral or written, become true examples of self-expression.

Composition may be classified according to whether it is (*a*) free or (*b*) translation from the mother tongue; (1) oral or (2) written. All four kinds of composition have their legitimate uses under the direct method. Generally speaking, "free" composition comes before translation, oral work before written, but for the first six months there is little writing and very little translation[3].

Until the fifth form is reached by far the greater part of the composition is oral, although an exercise worked through orally is often written out afterwards to impress it upon the memory. For this procedure there are three reasons. Languages are tongues, so much so that we call one that is no longer spoken a "dead" language.

[1] J. L. Paton in *The Teaching of Classics in Secondary Schools in Germany*, pp. 156, 157.

[2] This point has been well worked out by S. O. Andrew in the first part of his *Praeceptor*.

[3] This remark applies only to Latin. In the case of Greek, which is begun later, the procedure is rather different.

Therefore, to speak a language and to hear it spoken help us to understand it and the literature written in it. Secondly, oral work is rapid, and so saves much valuable time. Thirdly, by oral work the teacher can correct a boy's errors before they are perpetuated by being committed to paper. As far as possible, only correct work is written, and *littera scripta manet.*

The first principle of teaching classical composition is to form habits of correct expression instead of setting traps for the unwary. Little by little the pupil must be made to "feel his feet" until accuracy becomes instinctive. Confidence, the sense of power and mastery, is not only a test of progress but also the best possible stimulus to interested effort. The motto "thorough" again comes to the mind. In accordance with this principle the earliest exercises will be very simple. They will consist for several weeks mainly of answers to easy questions and commands. For example:

Master. Surge. *Boy.* Surgo.

Master. Specto ianuam. Quid facio? *Boy.* Spectas ianuam.

Master. Quid specto? *Boy.* Ianuam spectas.

Master (looking at the window). Quid nunc specto? *Boy.* Fenestram spectas.

Master. Ubi iacet liber? *Boy.* In mensa liber iacet.

Master. Quid in ludo agimus? *Boy.* Discimus, recitamus, scribimus in ludo.

To encourage confidence in the weaker brethren the answers may be given first by a bright pupil, then by all in chorus, and finally by a dull member of the class. If the answers are written, it will be upon the black-board, either by the master or by a clever boy. It will be a reward for smartness to assign the task of writing to the first boy to be ready with a correct answer. During the first few weeks other written work will be seldom given; perhaps once a week an exercise will be written out on paper by all, but only after it has been thoroughly mastered orally. These exercises will be returned the next day, before the problems presented by them have been forgotten, with the mistakes struck out but not corrected. The corrections should be made by the pupils themselves.

Variety is added to the oral work by giving a bright boy the duties of master, and making him ask the questions and give the commands. With a little practice the better boys imitate their teacher very well, and after a while even the dullards become tolerably expert at "playing master."

Examples of such exercises as the above will be found in any of the direct method courses for the first year. As time goes on the short sentences of which they are composed ought to be combined into continuous narratives, the master showing the way by means of a few models which the boys are to imitate.

Here is an example. It is of a particularly useful kind, as it is an expression in words of a boy's experience, and the great aim of the direct method is to bring language teaching into touch with reality.

Magister intrat. Discipuli fortasse ludunt. Itaque magister "Nolite ludere," inquit, "tacete et spectate me." Pueri tacent et magistrum spectant dum docet linguam Latinam.

Narratives such as this may be lengthened as the class gains confidence and a sense of power, but from first to last they should be repeated by several boys (sometimes with a change of person, e.g. "Nos fortasse ludimus," to insure variety) until they are known by heart, and then finally written out, either on the black-board or, if the class be ready for such an exercise, by each boy on paper. *Hear, repeat, write*—this motto is an excellent summary of the first stages of classical composition. In its broad outlines Greek composition will resemble Latin in the earlier stages, but as Greek is begun two years later than the sister tongue, when considerable progress has been made in one ancient language, while the intellect is much more developed, less time is necessary for the preliminary steps, and written work can come earlier and more frequently.

Occasionally, though not during the first fortnight, a few English sentences may be set for translation, not to teach rules, but to drive them home, and to afford a test of progress. These should be done orally before being written out on the black-board or on paper.

As soon as the class have begun a continuous reader, the composition will naturally be based upon the contents of that reader. Vocabulary and grammar should be, as far as possible, the same in composition as in reading, and the kinds of exercise which combine these two sides of the work include the following:

(1) A story in the reader may be re-told with a change of tense, of person or of number. This is an easy exercise, more adapted to oral than to written work.

(2) Sections of the story may be summarised by the boys with or without books. With a little instruction and encouragement from the teacher most boys do this task very creditably, and in one school the practice is continued until the end of the school course. The habit is quickly formed of making a mental *précis* of what one is reading, and, once formed, this habit is obviously useful, not only

for storing the mind with words, phrases and constructions, but also for strengthening the powers of attention and concentration. The summaries may be oral, written or both.

(3) Occasionally the story lends itself to dramatisation. "The first 150 odd lines of the second *Aeneid* are easily cast into dramatic form; the story of Sinon is pretended to be true, Ulixes and Calchas plot together, a messenger goes off to Delphi to consult the oracle of Apollo; the master's desk serves as the Trojan horse, Laocoon and Capys make their speeches over it, and then the Trojan shepherds enter dragging Sinon, who is led to Priam and tells him his story[1]." Such exercises as this come naturally to boys trained on the direct method from the first, but boys not accustomed to act in class are not only shy but have great difficulty in composing complete sentences conforming to grammatical rules.

(4) A piece of English, based upon the Latin or Greek text, may be dictated by the master and then translated by the class, first orally and then in writing.

Two other kinds of composition should be noticed here—reproduction and free composition based on pictures.

Reproduction means the repetition by the learner of narrative already learnt, and its most common form is when the teacher tells a story, explaining, in Latin or Greek, each sentence as he goes along, asking questions, still in Latin or Greek, to determine whether points are understood, and then having the story repeated, sentence by sentence and afterwards as a whole, by several boys in turn. Finally the story is written out by all, perhaps as home-work.

[1] R. B. Appleton, *Suggestions*, p. 40. See also *The School World* for September, 1912.

Later on in this book two examples of such lessons will be given, so that there is no need now to enter into elaborate detail, but one general warning will be very much in place. Lessons of this kind, to be successful, must be systematically graduated. They begin with quite easy, short sentences—brief jokes or anecdotes—the meaning of which no one can fail to grasp, and the narratives gradually increase in length and difficulty until fair facility is attained. It is found that complex sentences of any length are bound to prove a stumbling-block at first, and it is suggested that such sentences may be split up into their component parts and presented paratactically, as soon as they have been read out in their syntactical form. To master the complex sentence and the period is extremely important, and no effort should be spared so to impress their characteristics upon the learner's mind that he may come not only to understand idiomatic speech, but also to speak and write idiomatically.

Obviously the narrative need not be reproduced exactly as it was given by the teacher. Almost infinite variety is possible, from a brief *précis* to a lengthy amplification. The utmost scope is thus given to any originality the boys may have, and to the literary talent that is sure to be found in some of them. Deviations from the original, however, are not to be encouraged at first. Considerable practice in imitation, almost slavish imitation, is necessary before original composition is in any way feasible. Step by step, little by little, precept upon precept—all these mottoes apply to the direct as much as to any other method. But in time greater freedom is attained, until original essays are by no means impossible feats. Last year a Perse boy of fourteen who had been learning Latin for three years, wrote and published a very creditable *In Caesarem Gulielmum Oratio*. A few paragraphs from this are reprinted in the Appendix.

Composition based on pictures was first described in *The School World* for July, 1904, from which the following account is taken. Twelve series of pictures, of the sort described below, are published by the De la More Press under the title *Latin Picture Stories*. They would serve almost equally well for Greek.

The repugnance felt by a child to a Latin declension is due to his ignorance of its nature and use. Even when the few English declensions (*who*, *whom*, *whose*, and the like) are familiar, and some progress has been made in French, there is still something mysterious and unmeaning in *mensa*, *mensa*, *mensam*, and the rest of the rigmarole. The present writer well remembers the state of perplexity which followed his being informed that *mensa* could mean "O table." What manner of people might these strange folk be who spoke to their tables? Surely something can be done to put more meaning into the lifeless forms. If the class be shown models or pictures of Roman soldiers, and then be told, with translation if necessary, *Hic gladius est ; miles gladium habet ; mucro gladii acutus est*, and so on, the child-mind will after a while be prepared to learn the paradigm and the names of the cases that compose it. Of course it is not intended that the process should be prolonged. As soon as the child understands what a paradigm is, he may learn similar paradigms at once. A paradigm is a shorthand summary of certain facts of language. When these facts are understood, but not before, the shorthand is an aid to memory. If a declension be learnt before the meanings of the cases, it may be repeated parrot-wise, but the knowledge is useless, for it cannot be applied. It is as well, however, to prevent the impression that pictures are meant to be an easy and rapid road to a knowledge of Latin. On the contrary, the difficulties must be faced, the paradigms learnt.

But it is equally necessary that they should be learnt intelligently.

Another use of pictures and models is to serve as material for composition. Ordinary illustrations will often suffice, but they may be specially prepared for the purpose. Series of pictures, representing the chief moments of a story, have been successfully used in modern-language teaching, and there is no reason why they should not be equally serviceable to the classical master. Under careful guidance a class may learn, by working with their teacher, the laws they must obey in writing a piece of composition. The following are short descriptions of a series of six pictures used by the present writer for this purpose:

I. Sextus Tarquinius being flogged.

II. The people of Gabii welcome him.

III. Sextus sends a messenger to his father.

IV. Tarquinius Superbus strikes off the tallest poppy heads.

V. The chief men of Gabii are led away to death or exile.

VI. The Romans enter and take possession of the city.

Now it is obvious that the pictures in this case cannot give the whole of the story. No one can tell, unless he is familiar with the legend, that the gentleman in IV, striking down the poppies, is the Roman king, and father of the gentleman in I who is receiving the flogging. So at some point or other in the lesson the teacher must impart such information as is absolutely necessary.

If the class consists of boys in their second or third year of Latin, the lesson takes somewhat the following form. The class looks at the first picture, and then the master asks about whom they are going to talk. Answer: *Sextus Tarquinius*. Teacher: "What are you going to say about him?" The question may be asked in Latin if it be thought advisable. Answer: *Verbera patitur*. Teacher: *Cur verbera patitur?* Answer: *Ut Gabinos fallat*. It may happen that a boy will suggest the addition of *sua sponte* or *iussu patris*, or even the prefixing of *Cum Romani Gabios vi expugnare non possint*. Perhaps no boy is ready with an answer, or the answer given is imperfect. The teacher must then suggest an answer, or bring about the amendment of the faulty one. He must pay attention to the order of words, and show how the order of words is, roughly speaking, the order of thought. Plenty of scope is thus given to his ingenuity and power of stimulating interest. When the first picture is finished the final description is written on the blackboard, thus:

Cum Romani Gabios vi expugnare non possint, Sextus Tarquinius, filius Superbi, sua sponte verbera patitur ut Gabinos fallat.

Picture II.

T. About whom are we going to talk?
A. *Gabini* (teacher suggests *illi*).
T. *Quid faciunt Gabini?*
A. *Sextum excipiunt* (teacher suggests *eum*).
T. *Quando excipiunt?*
A. *Volneribus visis.*
T. *Quomodo?*
A. *Laeti.*

In this way the second sentence is composed. *Illi volneribus visis eum laeti excipiunt.* And the story might go on: *Tandem imperio summo potitus Sextus epistulam ad patrem mittit ut discat quid sit faciendum. Ille veritus ne infidus sit nuntius nihil voce respondet, sed in hortum progressus summa capita papaverum baculo decutit. Quibus renuntiatis Sextus ubi intellegit quid pater velit primores aut occidit aut expellit. Deinde bonis occisorum populo divisis placet ut Romani Gabiis potiantur.*

The whole story is then copied from the board by each boy into an exercise book kept for the purpose. As each boy has a copy of the pictures, and, so to speak, sees the events taking place before his eyes, it is natural to have the story told in the present tense, as above. Afterwards (e.g. as home-work) it can be written out in the past. This will involve attention to sequence of tenses, to the difference between perfect and imperfect, and so on. Other variations are possible. Sextus may tell the story, or Tarquin the Proud, or the people of Gabii. Later on more advanced pupils may compose original themes without help, but at first these must be avoided. If allowed a free hand young boys will simply evade difficulties.

The chief value of such a lesson as the one outlined above is its elasticity, and the consequent possibilities of hearty co-operation between teacher and class. By working with his pupils the teacher shows them how they ought to work by themselves. At the same time he is prepared to welcome any suggestion and turn it to the best advantage. The "average boy," who often sinks into listless apathy after a few terms at translation exercises he does not quite understand, is roused to action when he sees his teacher working with him and leading him to the achievement of something artistic. And all the while the connection between words and ideas is kept alive by the use of visual-impressions, instead of words, to suggest the ideas to be clothed in a Latin dress, an excellent antidote for the mechanical, word-for-word operation into which translation is apt to degenerate. There is no opportunity for the learner to mistake what he has to express in Latin. In a picture all is clear-cut and precise. Finally, that capture of the attention by the illustration, a serious drawback during a construing lesson, is a positive virtue when the details of the illustration form the subject which the pupils have to turn into Latin.

Illustrations, then, may be used in the very first period of Latin teaching to familiarise the child with inflexions, as a preliminary to the learning of paradigms, by making him connect inflected forms with various relations coming within his sense-experience. At a later stage pictures and picture-stories may be used as material for composition. During both periods something is being done to enlarge the learner's stock of Roman ideas, and so help him to reconstruct the life of the people whose language he is studying. It may be added that, much of the work being *viva voce*, progress is more rapid than when composition is taught by writing alone.

These few remarks are the outcome of the writer's personal experience. He has used pictures with three forms representing three stages of development, and the results are even better than he expected. Too much is not claimed for them, but any plan is worth a trial which promises to make progress in Latin easier and more sure.

§ 4. VERSES.

Verse composition is studied by University scholarship candidates only, as no good comes from forcing boys with no gift for versification laboriously to put together tags that happen to scan. Even at the older Universities verses are no longer a compulsory subject for honours candidates, and in time schools may be affected by the recent changes in the tripos regulations at Cambridge. But at the present time nearly all scholarship candidates offer verses, and this is as it should be. The practice not only increases appreciation of ancient poetry, but impresses upon the young mind the value of literary form, to say nothing of the fact that it affords a very pleasant occupation.

The old method of verse-making has nothing to recommend it but its thoroughness. Dull, mechanical, unintelligent, it condemns itself, and besides, it is not based upon the only sure foundation—a patient study of Sophocles, Virgil and Ovid. The pupil cannot make bricks without clay; he must read his models again and again until he is quite familiar with their peculiarities; he must declaim long passages and learn some hundreds of lines by heart; then, and then only, is he ready to begin writing verses himself. No piecing together of fragments, however systematic, however long practised, can make up for the loss of this indispensable preliminary.

The old method, too, besides being inefficient, is sadly wasteful of time. Years of painful diligence often result in nothing but boredom and annoyance. Conscious of no progress, vaguely aware that something is wrong, without in the least knowing what is the matter, the pupil reaches at last that hopeless condition when he neither learns nor wishes to learn.

Such is the intellectual state that the direct method never allows to develop. The willing co-operation of the learner, won by never setting him a task beyond his powers, by following the psychologically correct order of presentation, by his consciousness of progress, by his understanding the reason for the various steps in the course, while realising that effort is certain to be crowned with success, is rarely absent except in the case of boys with no literary tastes, and all such should give up their classics long before the stage when verses are begun.

If the principles stated above are not sound, how is it that a University student of fair ability, after a careful examination of models and some practice, finds no difficulty in composing Latin lyrics and hendecasyllables or Greek elegiacs? So our tiro in versification must first read large portions of (say) Ovid, and learn by heart about two hundred lines. He must learn the rules of scansion and versification, and have them copiously illustrated from his reading, until one day his master suggests that they should compose a few couplets. A subject is chosen; perhaps it is a joke, or an anecdote, or a stanza of simple poetry. Step by step a version is worked out, the master leading, the others following or even suggesting, until the whole is complete. Then a similar task is set to be done without help. This is almost certain to result in a crop of blunders (although some versions may be quite good), and the correction of these convinces all that a certain amount of disciplined drill is essential. So a text-book is taken and a few typical exercises are worked. After about a month their purpose has been served, and stories, epigrams and simple translations are resumed until a fair standard of accuracy and fluency has been attained. Iambics are approached in a similar manner, but Latin hexameters, in spite of their difficulty, will not need text-book drill. A few demonstration lessons are all that is required. It may be noticed in passing that only Latin elegiacs, the type of verse usually attempted by immature pupils, claim any large number of text-books, and this shows, if proof were needed, that all kinds of versification should be postponed until late in the course, when text-books are scarcely needed at all.

One set of verses in both languages every week for a year or eighteen months will bring any likely pupil well up to University scholarship standard. Not all of these should be of the usual kind; original composition, the subjects being of topical interest, may be done occasionally, and a word is not out of place in defence of epigrams. The writer has found that the majority of boys take a great delight in attempting them, and no other form of exercise inculcates to the same degree the literary virtues of point, brevity and conciseness.

§ 5. GRAMMAR.

The direct method does not imply, as many opponents still think, that grammar is to be neglected. But the term "grammar" may have two very different meanings. It may refer to the science of grammar, the aim of which is to discover, for the mere love of the discovery, the laws of speech; or it may mean the learning of certain convenient formulae in order to facilitate the correct use of speech. In other words, certain results of grammatical science are of practical value. It is with these results, these summaries of facts, that the direct method is concerned. Grammar is its ally, not an object of worship. It may be that this modicum of grammar has, in itself, educational value; it will certainly be a good foundation for the scientific study of grammar later on. But of this the direct method, as such, takes no account. Its object is command of a language—power to understand it, power to use it—and no subsidiary aims must distract it from its purpose. What, then, are the limits which are to be imposed upon grammatical study?

Firstly, grammar is learnt as required. When a pupil feels the need of a grammatical rule, when he realises the meaning of a paradigm or formula, then, and then only, is the new information given. So studied, grammar is a help, not lumber. It follows at once that the order in which the various sections of the grammar are studied is not necessarily the order in which they occur in a grammatical text-book. Verbs may be needed before nouns, the third conjugation before the first. If so, there is no reason why the parts wanted should not be learned out of their usual or logical order. Afterwards, when the ground has been covered, and the time has come for revision, the traditional arrangement should be observed. It is as convenient for revision as it is inconvenient when the beginner is meeting new forms for the first time. Similarly with syntax; a construction may be used if it satisfies a real want, even though it may occur late in the ordinary grammars. Of course, this principle has its limits. It would be very unwise to introduce final clauses to a beginner ignorant of indicative tenses. All that is now claimed is that no grammatical form or construction, if wanted, should be postponed merely because it is usually introduced later. This applies to both Latin and Greek, although it is during the earlier Latin lessons that one is most conscious of the value of freedom in respect of order.

When learning grammar, young pupils may fail to grasp the meaning of what they are doing. The teacher, therefore, must be particularly careful to prevent mechanical, unintelligent memorising. The parrot-like repetition of a declension, without any rational comprehension of the meaning of the cases, used to be the commonest fault in language-teaching, and it is by no means extinct even now. Teachers hoped that intelligent meanings would in time attach themselves to inflected forms unintelligently learnt. The more gifted pupils may progress satisfactorily in these conditions, but the rank and file soon sink into helpless bewilderment. At the best, the process of learning is dull to a degree, and dulness is an insuperable barrier to steady improvement. In order to be appreciated, a paradigm or grammatical rule should appear to be the inevitable outcome of facts already learnt, a convenient summary of past experience. Hence examples should come before a rule, that the latter may have something to which it may appeal. To complete the process the rule should be applied in composition, either oral or written.

It should be noticed that the acceptance of the above principle does not involve a laborious preparation for each new paradigm. It involves such a preparation for one paradigm, e.g. for the first declension; but when the meaning of a declension has been clearly understood, then other declensions may be learnt by rote without any ill results. Greek grammar scarcely requires any propaedeutic at all, or, to put the matter more exactly, experience of Latin paradigms and formulae paves the way to similar generalisations in a closely related language.

Beginners should not be troubled with rare exceptions. These can be learnt as they occur in the course of reading; there is no need to practise them of set purpose. The beginners' sphere of action is the commonplace. But the commonplace may be very irregular, and mere difficulty should not prevent useful information being presented at an early stage. And although nothing but the essentials should be committed to memory, the minimum, the framework into which further details may be fitted, must be thoroughly mastered. Hazy notions, imperfectly remembered paradigms, half-understood rules, are infinitely worse than complete ignorance. The latter can easily be remedied, while the former tend to become stereotyped as vicious mental habits.

Two grammatical text-books will be required during the course. The first will be a brief summary of the accidence and syntax learnt during the first two years. It will be committed to memory, and forms a suitable appendix to the second-year reader. A part of it may appear at the end of the first Latin book, while the first-year Greek course will probably contain the whole of the

Greek grammar required for practical purposes, as in the case of Greek an effort is made to cover in one year the ground that requires two years of Latin. The second text-book is for reference only, and there are several larger school grammars which answer the purpose. The short grammar should, if possible, be entirely in Latin or Greek.

During the first few weeks, or even months, there is no need for special grammar lessons. Each period contains a great amount of grammar learnt *pari passu* with the use of forms, and no good service is performed by separating grammar from the context from which it derives its life and reality. But later on, perhaps in the second year of Latin and in the third term of Greek, when the pupils have made some definite progress, and are thus prepared to be interested, a series of lessons should be given on important points. These will be in English, and will deal with, e.g. the meaning of "grammatical rule," inflexion as an aid to expression, analytic and synthetic languages, the imperfections of Latin and Greek inflexions, Latin and Greek constructions in *oratio obliqua*, the various ways of expressing the idea of "purpose" in Latin or Greek, the main uses of cases, tenses, moods. One lesson every fortnight will suffice, and the practice may be continued to the end of the school course. This teaching is intended to be a foundation for the study of scientific grammar in the sixth form or at the University. If carefully prepared, and adapted to the pupil's stage of development, the lessons will be found not only profitable but also exceedingly interesting.

All school grammars are best interleaved, so that striking illustrations of rules which occur in the reading lesson may be inserted in their proper place.

CHAPTER IV

DETAILS

§ 1. Text-Books.

A few words must be said about text-books and their use. Suitable dictionaries have yet to be written, but the teacher on the direct method has now a fair choice of "courses" for the first and second years. Those which appeared during the earlier period of the reform movement do not reject translation, but merely supplement it by exercises of a different type. These are questions put in the foreign language to be answered in the foreign language, and sentences with missing words or missing endings to be supplied by the learner. This class includes Scott and Jones' *First Latin Course*, W. H. S. Jones' *First Latin Book*, and Professor E. A. Sonnenschein's *Ora Maritima* and *Pro Patria*. Later works apply the direct method with greater strictness, translation being either omitted altogether or reduced to a minimum. Such are Paine and Mainwaring's *Primus Annus*, Granger's *Via Romana*, Appleton and Jones' *Initium* and *Pons Tironum*.

The last-mentioned book is intended to bridge the passage from the first year to the second; books specially for the second year are rare, *Puer Romanus*, by the same authors, being the only one strictly adhering to the direct method. Plays are now common enough, but mention need be made of only two collections, one for the first year (*Decem Fabulae*) by Paine, Mainwaring and Ryle, and one for the second (*Perse Latin Plays*) by Appleton and Jones.

It is customary now to mark all the long vowels in text-books for at any rate the first year.

There is no satisfactory first Greek course, for Dr Rouse's book, published by Blackie, is not sufficiently direct in method, but the same author's *Greek Boy at Home* is an admirable reader, and may for the present be used with any Greek grammar. It is to be hoped that a first Greek book on direct lines will soon be written. Dr Rouse's dialogues from Lucian, published by the Oxford University Press, make good reading for the second year, and Greek notes are attached.

For the third and fourth years of Latin, and for the second year of Greek, the readers should consist of a plain text, or, if notes and vocabulary are added, they should be in the ancient language. The latter are scarce, but the former include, besides the well-known Oxford and Teubner texts, the cheap series of Latin texts, with all the long vowels marked, published by Messrs Blackie.

When using a first or second year course the teacher must always remember that, while system is essential for steady progress, the text-book is not to be slavishly followed. He must be prepared to omit or postpone a section, to alter it materially so as to meet the special needs of his class, or to introduce a new point in his own way if circumstances suggest a suitable mode of so doing. The direct method means elasticity, adaptability, the spirit as opposed to the letter, and can be successfully applied by nobody who fails to associate the work with the daily and hourly experience of his pupils. A boy at the beginning of the second year may mutter an indistinct reply. Here is the master's opportunity. He should retort: "Mussitas, Quinte; nescio quid dicas," and go on briefly to indicate, by further examples, the mood of the verb in dependent questions, and this preliminary discussion may possibly take the place of a section in the textbook; it will certainly be at any rate an admirable preparation for it. Obviously no detailed rules for the teacher's guidance can be given; he must master the principle, and then work out the applications of it for himself.

§ 2. VOCABULARIES AND DICTIONARIES.

The teacher on the direct method explains all new words, as far as possible, without the use of the mother tongue. Vocabularies with English equivalents are a great nuisance, because pupils get hold of them to facilitate the preparation of their home-work, and in this way undo the good of the last lesson and perhaps of other lessons as well. One of the greatest needs of to-day is a Latin-Latin dictionary of small bulk, similar to Smith's small Latin-English dictionary. The sixth form can use Forcellini (Latin edition), or, if copies of this are not available, Lewis and Short can do them no harm, since after four or five years of the direct method the habit of thinking in the ancient language is fully developed, and cannot be broken by occasional references to Latin-English equivalents. For the first few terms vocabularies must be made by the teacher to suit the needs of his class, and the writer of a text-book must either write a vocabulary to fit the text, or else leave explanations entirely to the class teacher. The latter is the ideal way, but some teachers prefer to have help at the end of the book. What has been said above applies, *mutatis mutandis*, to Greek.

Whether the text-book he employs contains a vocabulary or not, the teacher will be obliged to train himself to paraphrase readily and accurately in the ancient languages. Unless the teacher has this power his teaching cannot be a success, and may be a bad failure. Of course the greatest difficulty occurs during the earliest lessons, when the learner's stock of words is very small; after a few months the task becomes much easier. It will perhaps be useful to describe briefly all the various ways of explaining a new word to a class.

In some cases the word can be directly associated with a thing or an action. There can be no difficulty in explaining the nouns *mensa*, *stilus*, *fenestra*, *tectum*, *digitus*, *oculus*, *gena*; the adjectives *magnus*, *parvus*, *altus*, *albus*, *candidus*, *ruber*, *durus*, *mollis*; the pronominal adjectives *hic*, *ille*, *alius*, *alter*, *neuter*, *nullus*; the prepositions *in*, *sub*, *de*, *ex*, *cum*, *sine*, *ante*, *post*, *ad*, *contra*; the verbs *surgo*, *teneo*, *habeo*, *ambulo*, *claudo*, *aperio*, *tollo*, *mitto*, *clamo*. All these words, and a considerable number of others, can be clearly explained by a gesture or a little dramatic action. In this way a start is made.

Many other words and phrases can be explained by pictures. *Villa*, *aratrum*, *miles*, *scutum*, *pilum*, *toga*, are examples of words which come under this class.

Possibly most are best explained by a paraphrase. E.g. "*humilis* est contrarium adiectivi *altus*," or, "*arare* est verbum, et *aratrum* est nomen instrumenti," or, "*facetiae*, sermo qui nobis risum moveat."

As the teacher must be quite ready to paraphrase accurately, even on the spur of the moment, he ought thoughtfully to devise plans to improve his power of interpretation, and to spare no pains in actual practice. A paraphrase is not a logical definition, but it has to be carefully worded and as accurate as thought can make it.

Difficult as the process is, it is not nearly so difficult as the problems which meet the supporter of English equivalents when he is brought face to face with words like *ratio* or *καθίστημι*. The most troublous times occur during the first few weeks, when the boys are still very limited in their vocabularies, and the master is often barred from an admirable explanation, because it introduces a construction beyond the present stage of development. But there are helps to lessen these difficulties; paraphrase can be combined with pictures and dramatic action. Dramatic action will explain the adverbs in:

Bene scribo; nunc male scribo,

and the knowledge thus acquired can be used to explain the corresponding adjectives by means of a paraphrase, e.g.:

Is bonus est qui bene agit; is malus est qui male agit.

Puto or *cogito* can be explained by assuming an attitude of thought, to be followed by the remark:

Dum cogito, taceo.

Pictures are at least as useful in combination with paraphrase as dramatic action. Explain *animal* by a drawing, and there can follow at once:

Canis est animal quod *au, au,* latrat;

and

Avis est animal quod per aëra volat. Nonnullae aves canere sciunt.

A picture of corn suggests:

Ex frumento facimus panem;

Frumentum dum in agro stat est seges.

The picture explains *frumentum,* and from this paraphrases

explain *panis* and *seges*. To be able to sketch, to be a lively actor—these are invaluable aids to the teacher, be his classical attainments what they may.

Words taught in this way are not divorced from their context but associated with concrete experience. They are alive, and not merely mechanical sounds. The English word may, indeed, suggest itself, or it may even be given by the teacher, but it will come after the direct association has done its beneficent work. The mental process, once performed, cannot be undone, and the good results remain.

A few words may be connected with English equivalents, either because a paraphrase is too difficult, or because the teacher cannot think of a suitable one on the spur of the moment. A faulty paraphrase does obvious harm, and time is more valuable than a strict adherence to the canons of even the direct method. Instances of such words are *honestus*, *certus*, *auxilium*, *officium*, *credo*, *oportet*.

But undoubtedly the best possible explanation of a word is a skilfully prepared context. There is so much of the meaning of words that depends upon their context—which is, as it were, the source of their vitality—that no better service could be done to a boy than to train him to look to it, instead of regarding words as separate entities with meanings independent of their neighbours. A good teacher will use this method to the utmost, and give many explanations of the type "pietatem boni parentibus, patriae, deis praestant."

Turning to the learner's side of the question, we notice that everyone's mental equipment comprises two kinds of vocabulary—a list of words understood, but rarely if ever used, and a list of words both understood and in regular use. The former is always greater than the latter; yet the latter is by far the more important, and every effort ought to be made to increase it. Now we learn to use words only by using them, and this truth shows that the direct method, which relies so much upon self-expression, has in this respect a great advantage over its competitor. In the later stages of the classical course, in the sixth form and at the University, definite steps should be taken to make the acquisition of a working vocabulary regular and systematic.

§ 3. Conversational Phrases.

The teacher would do well to become familiar with a few words and phrases which, although they do not in every case occur frequently in ancient literature, yet help to complete the Roman or Greek atmosphere. Any interruption of the lesson by English words is unwise, and unpleasant to the ear. For this reason the pupils should be re-named. Greek names are plentiful enough, but there are not enough *praenomina* to go round a large class. Some English surnames lend themselves readily to inflexions, and these supply a few deficiences; "Flack" becomes Flaccus or Φλάκκος, "Jones" appears as Iunius or Ἴων. Again, a personal peculiarity, or the suggestiveness of an English surname, will often solve a difficulty; "King" is Rex or Βασιλεύς, a budding poet is Vergilius or Ὅμηρος. A little thought will soon provide everyone with a new appellation.

The routine of the classroom, and the furniture it contains, do not cause much trouble. *Mensa, sella, fenestra, ianua, stilus, charta, tabula nigra, creta, pandere, claudere, purgare,* τράπεζα, θύρα, θυρίς, ἡ γύψος, σανίς, *ἀνοιγνύναι, κλῄειν, καθαίρειν* are among the many which occur to the mind almost at once.

More difficult to use readily, though perfectly familiar to even mediocre scholars, are the phrases which are needed for praise or blame, for encouragement or exhortation. Greek is richer in such phrases than Latin, and in particular, many Greek particles and their combinations are best taught when some class incident makes their use natural and easy. For example, suppose a boy comes in suddenly with a message from another master, the teacher may say *καὶ μὴν πάρεστιν Εὐριπίδης*. A wrong answer may be given: *ὦ παῖ, κακὸς εἶ, κάκιστος μὲν οὖν*, or *τί δὴ ἀπεκρίνω;* A few examples are now given of phrases and exclamations which may prove useful. But the teacher must think of many others for himself, and employ them when the occasion invites.

Salvete, valete.
Animum attende.
Perge recitare.
Noli mussitare.
Noli cum vicino colloqui.
Clara voce.
Aliter verte; expone aliis usus vocabulis.
Incipe, parve puer.
Hoc age; hoc agite.
Quid significat...?
Quid agis?
Liquetne?
Quota pagina? Quotus versus?
Erravisti, Tite. Quid dicendum erat?
Quid debuit Titus dicere?
Quid ad rem?
O di immortales (at anything surprising).

O stultissimos!
O puerum valde immemorem!
I in malam rem!
It clamor caelo (at a noise).
Monstrum horrendum informe ingens (of a "howler").
Ludus a non ludendo (a boy does not attend).
Punctum (mark).
χαίρετε.
πρόσεχε τὸν νοῦν.
ἑρμήνευε Ἑλληνιστί, Ῥωμαϊστί, Ἀγγλιστί.
λαβὲ τὴν γύψον καὶ γράψον.
πρόιθι.
παῦε, παῦε.
μὴ διαλέγου.
οὐκ ἂν φθάνοις προϊών (to a slow boy).
μὴ θορυβεῖτε, μὴ θορυβήσητε.
τί ἔδει λέγειν;
συνίημι, μανθάνω.
πόστη δέλτος; πόστος στίχος;
ποῖον ἔπος ἔφυγεν ἕρκος ὀδόντων;
οὐ φανερὸν τὸ....
ὦ Ζεῦ καὶ θεοί.
τί πρὸς τὸν Διόνυσον;
ὦ δυσμαθεῖς.
οἴμοι τῆς δυσμαθίας ὑμῶν.
οἴμοι τῆς λήθης σου.

Grammatical Terms.

Parts of speech: verbum, nomen, pronomen, adiectivum, adverbium, praepositio, coniunctio, exclamatio, supinum, gerundium, participium.

Cases: nominativus, vocativus, accusativus, genetivus, dativus, ablativus, locativus (casus).

Genders: masculinum, femininum, neutrum (genus).

Numbers: singularis, pluralis (numerus), or, singulariter, pluraliter.

Persons: prima, secunda, tertia (persona).

Tenses: praesens, futurum, imperfectum, perfectum, plus quam perfectum, futurum et perfectum (tempus).

Moods: indicativus, imperativus, subiunctivus, infinitivus (modus).

Voices: activa, passiva (vox), or, active, passive.

Degrees of Comparison: positivus, comparativus, superlativus (gradus).

Declinatio, coniugatio, declinare.

Parts of speech: *ῥῆμα, ὄνομα, ἀντωνυμία, ἐπίθετον, ἐπίρρημα, προθετικόν (πρόθεσις), σύνδεσμος, μετοχή.*

Cases: *ὀρθή, κλητική, αἰτιατική, γενική, δοτική (πτῶσις).*

Genders: *ἄρρεν, θῆλυ, οὐδέτερον (γένος).*

Numbers: *ἑνικός, δυαδικός (δυϊκός), πληθυντικός (ἀριθμός).*

Persons: *πρῶτον, δεύτερον, τρίτον (πρόσωπον).*

Tenses: *ἐνεστώς, μέλλων, ἀόριστος, παρατατικός, παρακείμενος, ὑπερσυντέλικος (χρόνος).*

Moods: *ὁριστική, προστακτική, ὑποτακτική, εὐκτική, ἀπαρέμφατος (ἔγκλισις).* Or use adverbs *ὁριστικῶς*, etc.

Voices: use (*ῥῆμα*) *ἐνεργητικόν, μέσον, παθητικόν*, or adverbs *ἐνεργητικῶς, μέσως, παθητικῶς*. "Voice" is *διάθεσις*.

Breathings: *ψιλή, δασεῖα (προσῳδία).*

Accents (*τόνοι*): *ὀξύτονος, παροξύτονος, προπαροξύτονος, περισπώμενος, προπερισπώμενος, βαρύτονος, ἄτονος, ἐγκλιτικός.*

Degrees of comparison: *θετικός, συγκριτικός, ὑπερθετικός (τρόπος).*

κλίσις, κλίνειν.

§ 4. ACTING.

Children love to act, and this natural instinct must not be neglected by the teacher of languages. The direct method encourages it from the very first, and the earliest lessons always consist of dramatic action accompanied by appropriate speech. Within a very few weeks simple dramatic pieces are understood and enjoyed. The teacher does well to compose dialogues adapted to the tastes and achievements of his class. These will be appreciated more than a play from a text-book, excellent as are the collections published during the last year or two. The pupils copy the words into note-books, either from dictation or from the black-board. Experience has shown that boys are often able to offer excellent suggestions for the structure of a play, although they may be unable to work out their suggestions in correct Latin or Greek. Here is a chance for co-operation between teacher and taught which greatly increases the likelihood of success. It may be remarked in passing that great care must be taken to supervise all that has been written into note-books. There are sure to be errors, and these must be corrected before they have been impressed upon the mind of the boy who committed them. If the teacher walk up and down among his pupils while the copying process is going on, he can easily detect blunders and omissions. The direct method demands that a learner should soon acquire the power of correct writing from dictation, and this is one reason among others why the restored pronunciation of Latin and Greek, which makes the script phonetic, should be adopted. Any system of pronunciation which does not distinguish between *ae* and *e*, *αι* and *ει*, is a source of disastrous confusion.

After the little play has been written out, it should first of all be studied in the same way as a portion of the reader. Then it should be acted, book in hand, those who have no part to take remaining seated. Finally the boys must learn the whole by heart, and act it without book, each boy having his turn in time. It thus becomes part of the repertoire of the class, to be acted on future occasions if it be thought desirable to do so. No scenery and no dresses are necessary; a few properties may be available, or a chair may represent a throne, a ruler a sword. But plays which prove popular may well be practised more thoroughly, with dress and properties, for occasions like Speech Day. Enjoyment is increased, and money saved, if boys and master co-operate to make, as far as possible, their own equipment.

Pupils who have made some progress take a great delight in trial scenes. With a little practice, and with one model to serve as a guide, these may be improvised with great pleasure and profit. A theft, a murder, a breach of contract—any offence or claim affords not only excellent opportunities for self-expression, but also a chance of teaching, in the best possible way, the customary procedure in an ancient law-court. No advantage is to be gained by giving details as to the steps the writer or his friends take to ensure success in these mock trials; the teacher himself must adopt such measures as seem best suited to his own peculiar requirements. The great essential is to encourage initiative and self-expression while discouraging disorder, frivolity, and mere chatter. It cannot be too urgently pleaded that the direct method leaves, and must leave, very much to the teacher's discretion, and also implies a teacher capable of exercising the highest kind of discipline, and pupils trained to employ themselves as rational creatures. If the old view obtains, that school is a place where pupils escape from a tyrant if they can, while the tyrant catches and punishes, if he can, the delinquents who rebel against his despotism, then the direct method will not, and cannot, succeed. Friendly relations, tempered by sincere respect, are essential postulates.

Sections of the ancient classics can easily be dramatised, either extempore or after due premeditation, when the original text has been thoroughly mastered. Reference to this has already been made in the section on composition, and it is sufficient here to insist upon the great value such a practice has in developing the dramatic instinct, and in encouraging intelligent self-expression.

§ 5. Realien.

For many years *realien* have been almost a superstition with teachers, and illustrated editions of the classics have appeared in great profusion. Lovers of the direct method have enthusiastically supported the new fashion, and everybody will admit that if we could only prepare a remote spot from which everything modern might be excluded—a restored *villa* inhabited by persons dressed in tunics and sandals—it would be a great help. But this cannot be done; Latin has to be taught within the four walls of a prosaic class-room. It is plain, therefore, that the classical teacher can make but little use of *realien*, and must strain every nerve to reconstruct the ancient world, not in a material sense, but in imagination. Material aids will not be despised; models and casts, whenever available, will be utilised to the full; pictures, accurately drawn, are wanted in great numbers. But too much importance must not be attached to these external helps. They must not be a substitute for failure to train and discipline the constructive imagination. It is difficult to hear with patience of boys who cannot read their Virgil, but delight to handle ancient coins or plaster casts of them. Such boys are either badly taught or else unfitted for a classical education. A means has been exalted into an end in itself. The study of antiques is not the study of the classics; it is not even a passable substitute for it. The one may help the other, but cannot replace it.

So the classical teacher, if he be true to his calling, will rely most upon illustrations, particularly upon restorations or pictures constructed from reliable archaeological *data*. It may, however, reasonably be doubted whether the ancient classical texts are the proper place for such pictures. The mind is very apt to be distracted from the work in hand by the presence of an illustration, and this danger is increased when the illustration does not bear immediately upon the text. But if (say) a first year reader contains a description of a Roman soldier, then a picture is not only useful, but almost necessary, because the written word is constantly appealing to some visual representation for its full comprehension.

Perhaps the very best use that can be made of pictures is to make them subjects for composition. The concentration of attention upon details is now no disadvantage but a distinct gain, because these details form the theme of our discourse.

The Association for the Reform of Latin Teaching has appointed a sub-committee for *realien*, and from its secretary[1] may be obtained information about the loan of coins, casts, photographs and so forth.

§ 6. Corrections.

If the direct method be adopted the teacher is saved a considerable amount of labour in correcting exercises, and so receives some slight compensation for the physical strain the system imposes, a strain which even the strongest feel for a time, until experience results in economy of effort, and the body adapts itself to new conditions. Not only is writing reduced to a minimum during the early part of the course, but the oral preparation of exercises diminishes appreciably the number of blunders committed. The mistakes, by the way, which do occur, are often of a different type from those common in the translation exercises that used to be universally practised, and might shock a master of the old school. But they quickly disappear, and it is certain that the usual schoolboy blunders, which often disfigure even fifth-form work, would amaze a master who has taught successfully on the direct method.

When mistakes are too many, or persist for too long a time, it means that the direct association has not been strong enough to counteract the boy's natural tendency to ignore endings which, in his eyes, are often unnecessary. The remedy is obvious—not more writing, but more direct association. Let the teacher return to the reader, with its accompaniment of question and answer, until the direct association has grown stronger. Then the written work will rapidly improve.

[1] S. E. Winbolt, Christ's Hospital, Horsham.

Any written exercise should always be promptly returned. Boys dislike their work to disappear, as it were, into empty space. The mistakes should be struck out or underlined, the corrections being made by the boys themselves, and only when they are at an utter loss must the master come to the rescue.

The best way to have corrections made is to take each boy individually. When the element of style comes in, as in the case of sixth-form work, no other way is possible. Time, however, is limited, and often a short address on the most instructive blunders in a batch of exercises, or a few words to each boy as his paper is returned, will be all that other portions of the work permit. Nevertheless, if only to inculcate thoroughness, once a month some particular exercise should be fully discussed with each boy separately.

§ 7. Some Difficulties and Dangers in applying the Direct Method.

Although the writer is convinced that classics can best be taught on the direct method, it is obvious that there are difficulties to be overcome and dangers to be faced. But the dangers at any rate are easily met; in fact, to be aware of their existence is to escape them.

Perhaps the greatest danger is lest the learner should become inaccurate. Much of the work is oral, and fluent readiness is encouraged as a means to rapid progress. There is accordingly a possibility that habits of inexactness may be formed through sheer carelessness. But against this there are efficient safeguards. Clear pronunciation must be insisted upon; mumbling, slurring of endings, hesitating speech of all kinds must be strictly suppressed;

grammatical inaccuracies must be checked whenever they occur. Mere prevention of error, however, is not sufficient. Every opportunity should be seized of practising correct Latin and Greek, both in chorus and by individual boys. Learning by heart of verse, proverbs, stories, simple dramatic scenes, is to be systematically encouraged. Above all, writing, after careful oral preparation, is the best precaution, although for the first week or two this writing is better done on the black-board by the pupils in turn, as in this way more careful attention is bound to be paid to accuracy. A word of warning is, however, necessary. Fluency is of such great importance that no plan must be adopted which militates against it. A pupil ought not to be interrupted in the middle of a sentence, certainly not in the middle of a spoken sentence. The correction should come immediately the sentence is finished. When corrected the sentence should be repeated, at least once, without any mistake. To impress the good is more important than to eliminate the bad. Besides grammatical inaccuracy, another kind of error may become common unless special attention be directed to its suppression. Pupils may habituate themselves to the making of straggling sentences, un-Latin or un-Greek in their loose structure, instead of forming a good prose style. There are two precautions to be taken. In the first place the master must supply good models, and make the class commit to memory passages typical of the style he wishes his pupils to imitate. Further, when some progress has been made (say in the fifth, or perhaps in the fourth, form) a few lessons may well be given, of course in English, on types of sentence-structure. These are followed by practice in the examination of examples taken from Cicero, Caesar, Thucydides and Demosthenes.

The chief types are not very numerous, and boys of fifteen readily understand and copy them.

The commonest fault of teachers who are new to the direct method is the tendency to speak too much themselves. Unconsciously, in fact, they use the class-room routine to improve their own command of spoken Latin and Greek, which they know is weak. But it cannot be too strongly urged that, within certain limits, the less the teacher speaks and the more his boys speak, the better for them both. In advanced classes of bright pupils the teacher is merely an umpire, appealed to when everyone else is at fault, the greater part of the work being carried on smoothly by the right persons, namely the pupils themselves. Such conditions, of course, do not occur at once, but imply a fairly long period of training and discipline. At first the pupils are not only ignorant but shy as well, and need to be encouraged to express their thoughts. Of all the expedients to meet this difficulty the most important is to train the learner from the very first to confess, by a *non intellego* or some such phrase, whenever he does not follow the course of the lesson. It is an understood thing that silence signifies comprehension. A boy is punished, not for ignorance, but for failure to acknowledge it openly. Without this convention the direct method must result in disaster. After a confession of ignorance a better informed boy is allowed to solve the problem, and the teacher does not give the answer until it is certain that nobody in the class is capable of doing so. A very useful plan, not easy with beginners, but quite feasible much earlier than would generally be supposed, is to set a boy to play the part of master. One of the brighter members of the class asks questions and gives commands to which the others have to respond.

Of course he makes mistakes, but the real master is on the spot to correct, criticise or suggest. All the class act the part in turn, the weaker boys last, when they have acquired experience and confidence by seeing their fellows succeed. Two advantages result from this plan. The questions and commands are not only heard but spoken by all, and the young "teacher" is put upon his mettle and stimulated to do his best. Very proud is he when he can conduct the class successfully without making any serious errors.

The freedom exercised by the teacher in the order of presentation must not be allowed to degenerate into chaotic licence. If a text-book be closely followed the danger disappears, but the more intelligent and enthusiastic a teacher is, the more he will attempt to work out schemes of his own. These efforts are in themselves entirely praiseworthy; nothing is so lifeless as slavish adherence to a book written on a method the very essence of which is spontaneity. Danger however occurs when the teacher forgets that a certain amount of new matter must be mastered each week, and that marking time is irksome to bright boys and stupefying to the others. Let the teacher, therefore, who wishes to be independent make out a scheme for himself, and follow it scrupulously.

Particular attention must be paid to discipline. Oral work is apt to be, and should be, lively, and the class must be kept well in hand. The boys are not to be suppressed; self-expression must be encouraged to the utmost. The technical skill of the teacher will be shown in directing this activity into its proper channels, in imposing restraint, in knowing just where to "draw the line," in controlling forces without weakening them, in displaying, in fact, the qualities of an ideal chairman.

His boys will be keen, alert, even self-assertive, but withal orderly and polite.

Finally, the teacher's own scholarship must stand the test of oral lessons. He is bound to make errors in speaking Latin and Greek, often without the slightest premeditation, but these errors must be gradually eliminated, until a fair standard of accuracy is acquired. He should not, however, be nervous, as his mistakes, if not too frequent or too glaring, produce no ill effects upon the boys' progress. Even young pupils not infrequently detect a slip, and call the master's attention to it. He need not be upset or ashamed. Let him exclaim, "O stultum magistrum! Magister ipse erro. Quis custodes custodiet ipsos?" and resolve to be more careful in future.

§ 8. Summaries.

During the fourth and fifth years of Latin (the second and third years of Greek) summaries of authors read in class form, together with translation into English, a very convenient kind of home-work. The boys are required to make the summary with their books closed, so that thorough preparation is necessary before beginning to write. It is not found that boys offend by referring to the original after they have begun to compose; if they do, the fault is easily detected from the character of the work.

For increasing command of idiom and vocabulary, for driving home the main points of the reading lesson, and for promoting the growth of the classical spirit, the plan is in every way admirable. Its full success, however, largely depends upon the training of the first three years. During that period the boys are systematically taught to make *précis* of what they read, and to recite them clearly, fluently and accurately, without reference to the text-book. Further training is afforded by the practice of reproducing, orally and in writing, a story told by the master. Without these preliminary exercises it is certain that such good results could not be obtained later on.

§ 9. VARIA.

In this section are grouped together a few odds and ends that cannot find a place elsewhere.

A boy taught on the direct method must obviously be able to write Latin and Greek accurately from dictation. If this habit is not readily acquired, special means should be adopted. The boys may be asked to write in turn phrases and sentences on the black-board until a reasonable degree of both facility and accuracy has been attained. Further practice will be obtained if the master dictate to the class the playlets he composes from time to time.

Marks may be given up in Latin or Greek so as to afford continuous practice in cardinal numerals; references to pages and lines offer an opportunity of using the ordinals. Dates may be written in Latin or Greek at the top of every written exercise.

CHAPTER V

THE FIRST YEAR OF LATIN

The first year of Latin is the most critical period in a boy's classical career. His mind may take a wrong bias; faulty teaching may create a violent dislike to the subject; early misconceptions may arrest progress and produce bewildered despair. Against all these contingencies the teacher must be on his guard, and lay a foundation which, however small, shall be firm and reliable. A certain, but limited, amount of knowledge has to be assimilated; interest has to be aroused, and a natural attitude towards the work encouraged and maintained. Above all, the sense of unreality must be banished; for a time Latin must be to the young beginner a living language, not different in kind from French.

Conscious of the importance of the stage with which he is dealing, the writer asks permission to put on record his own experience. He has taught beginners on the old method from old-fashioned text-books; he has followed the old lines substituting oral for written work; he has tried to combine direct and indirect teaching, and he has used the direct method pure and simple. On comparing the results he has no hesitation in deciding that the direct method, applied in a whole-hearted fashion, is by far the most satisfactory, and provides the surest foundation for future progress.

The scheme of work for the year is, roughly speaking, the simple sentence. It comprises the regular declensions and conjugations (except the subjunctive mood), the commoner case-usages and a vocabulary of about eight hundred words. New words are easily learnt at this stage. The time required is one period of three-quarters of an hour every day.

The direct method takes its material from three different sources:

(1) The pupil's own environment;

(2) Pictures;

(3) Books, both those specially written and those left us by the classical authors. Those specially written should be, as far as possible, classical in style and tone[1].

It is with (1) that the first lessons are most concerned. The class-room and its routine may, to an adult, appear trivial and uninteresting. But they are very real to a boy, and to connect language with reality is our primary object. At first the reality should be material and palpable; as time goes on other forms of reality will be made use of, until the ancient world at last loses its unreality and is reconstructed by continuous efforts of the imagination. Such a reconstruction is our ultimate aim, but the approach to it is gradual and difficult.

The writer and his colleagues have used many different types of text-books, and they have embodied the results of their experience in a recent work[2], but for the first dozen lessons or so no text-book at all should be used. For a fortnight no Latin ought to be seen before it has been heard and spoken. This psychological order—*hear*, *speak*, *see* or *write*—is the ideal one,

[1] The reader for the second year is best composed of easy and interesting portions of the classics connected by a modern setting classical in tone. *Puer Romanus* is an attempt to produce such a book.

[2] *Initium*, published by the Cambridge University Press.

and should be strictly observed at first. Later on it is impossible to keep to it except in the case of new constructions and of narratives told to be reproduced. By these stages does the infant learn his mother tongue, and the same mental processes are the natural ones for the beginner in a foreign language.

The first two lessons are in English, and give some account of the Romans, their place in civilisation, the Latin alphabet, pronunciation, accent and quantity. The writer has found it useful to add a third lesson, in which, after revision of previous work, he points out the force of order in such a sentence as:

Tom hits Jack.

He then goes on to observe that the same meaning could be secured (if -us were adopted as the sign of the subject and -um as that of the direct object) by:

Jackum hits Tomus;
or Jackum Tomus hits;
or Hits Tomus Jackum;

and so on, order being immaterial as far as sense is concerned[1]. In this way is the beginner introduced to inflexions.

The next lessons are so important that they are here printed almost *verbatim* from reports taken in September, 1914. But a printed account, however accurate, misses many essential points. It cannot give the minute care bestowed upon pronunciation, the exaggerated lengthening of all long syllables, the repetitions of words and phrases by the boys until they are said without stumbling. The lessons were given by the writer's colleague, Mr R. B. Appleton.

[1] It is convenient to point out here that in an inflected language order can be used to mark emphasis.

M. = master. P. = pupil.

M. (rising from his chair) *Surgo.* This is repeated once or twice.

M. (pointing at some bright boy) *Surge.* Boy rises, and master says *Surgis.*
This is repeated with other boys. Then the master turns to the rest of the class, and, pointing at a boy told to rise, says *Surgit.*

M. *Ego surgo.*
(pointing to boy) *Surge! Tu surgis;*
(looking at the class, but pointing to the boy) *Ille surgit.*
The class then repeat *Surgo,*
surgis,
surgit;
then *Ego surgo,*
tu surgis,
ille surgit.

M. (rising) *Quid facio?* The meaning of this was at once guessed from the intonation, and the correct answer *Surgis* came from several of the brighter boys.

M. *Bene! Tu surge! Quid facis?*

P. *Surgo.*

M. *Quid facit ille?*

Class. *Surgit.*
Then a boy is given a ruler and told in English to walk about the class, tell different boys to rise and ask them what they are doing. Thus we get:

P[1]. *Surge! Quid facis?*

P[2]. *Surgo.*

P[1]. *Quid facit ille?*

Class. *Surgit.*
This is repeated for several boys.

Then the master pointing at himself says *Ego sum magister.*

Then the master pointing at a boy says *Tu es puer.*

Then the master pointing at another boy says *Ille est puer.*

This is repeated; then the "surgo" business is gone through again with several questions such as *Quid facio? Quid facis?* thus preparing the way for

M. *Ego sum magister. Tu es puer. Ego sum magister. Quis sum?*[1]

P. *Magister es.*

M. *Ille est puer. Quis est ille?*

P. *Puer est ille.*

M. *Ego sum magister, non sum puer. Sumne puer?* The *ne* is not yet, of course, understood.

P. *Non.* This need not necessarily be objected to at first; later on *minime* can be substituted.

M. *Quis sum?*

P. *Magister es.*

M. (pointing to a boy) *Estne ille magister?*

P. *Non, ille est puer.*

M. *Sumne ego magister?* No reply is forthcoming because the Latin for "yes" is not known, so the master proceeds himself:

M. *Ita. Ego sum magister. Estne ille puer?*

P. *Ita. Ille est puer.*

The master then says to a boy, whom he takes out as before, but now speaking in Latin, *Tu es magister, ego sum puer. Dic "Surge" et "Quid facio?" et*

[1] The master should speak very clearly, very slowly and very deliberately. If he does so, few boys will fail to "pick up" e.g. the *es* required in the following answer.

"*Quid facis?*" One of the brightest boys must, of course, be chosen at first. He will walk about the room, and questions and answers such as the following will be made:

P[1]. *Surge! Quid facis?*

P[2]. *Surgo.*

P[1]. *Quid facit ille?*

Class. *Ille surgit.*

P[1]. *Estne ille magister?*

Class. *Non, ille est puer.*

And so on. If the boy-master makes a mistake, such as the omission of the *ne* in *Estne ille magister?* it is easy for the real master to prompt him.

N.B.—That different boys should thus take the part of master from the very earliest lessons is a point of extreme importance. Those who have not tried it can have no idea of the difference it makes both to accuracy and interest.

No English at all was spoken in this lesson until two minutes before the end, when the home-work was set. Henceforth it is to be understood that no English is spoken either by master or boys, unless the contrary is expressly stated.

Next lesson. Revision and plural of *surgo* and of *sum*.

M. (*placing a second chair to his own on the rostrum*) Beckons to a boy and says *Veni huc*, then *Sede*, and motions him down. The boy sits on the chair next to the master, who says to him, *Surge.* The master rises simultaneously with the boy, and addressing the class says, *Surgimus.*

This is repeated; then the master asks the class, *Quid facimus?* No answer is, of course, given, because the second person plural is not known, so the master prompts—*Surgitis.* Then again, *Nos surgimus. Quid facimus?*

Class. *Surgitis.*

M. (*addressing P¹ in class*) *Surge!* (*and to P²*) *Tu quoque surge!* As they rise the master says *Vos surgitis.* This is repeated with other boys. Then the master and the boy-master rise saying, *Nos surgimus. Quid facimus?*

Class. *Vos surgitis.*

The master, as before, tells two boys to rise and addressing the boy-master says, *Illi surgunt.* He repeats this with other boys and then asks the boy-master *Quid faciunt illi?*

Pm. *Illi surgunt.* [Pm is the boy-master.]

Repeat *Ego sum magister, tu es puer* etc. Then addressing Pm:

Ego sum magister et tu es magister; nos sumus magistri.

Then pointing to two boys,

Tu es puer et tu es puer; vos estis pueri.

Nos sumus magistri, vos estis pueri. Qui sumus nos?

Class. *Vos estis magistri.*

M. *Bene. Nos sumus magistri; vos estis pueri.* Then addressing Pm:

Nos sumus magistri; illi sunt pueri. Qui sumus nos?

Pm. *Nos sumus magistri.*

M. *Bene. Nos sumus magistri; illi sunt pueri. Qui sunt illi?*

Pm. *Illi sunt pueri.*

M. *Bene. Nos sumus magistri, illi sunt pueri.* Then addressing the class, *Qui estis vos?*

Class. *Pueri sumus.*

M. *Bene. Pueri estis. Qui sumus nos?*

Class. *Vos estis magistri.*

M. *Bene. Nos sumus magistri.* Then addressing P^{m}, but pointing to the class, *Illi sunt pueri.* This iterative style is, of course, deliberate; it is thus that the class is able to pick up the new forms. The master then takes chalk, and, writing on the board *Nos sumus magistri* asks *Quid facio?* No response, of course is given, and so the master prompts *Scribo.* He then gives the chalk to P^{m} and says *Scribe "Illi sunt pueri." Quid facis?*

P^{m}. *Scribo.*

M. *Ita. Scribis. Ego scribo et tu scribis.* Then pointing to P^{m}, but addressing a boy in the class, *Quid facit ille?*

P. *Ille scribit.*

M. *Bene. Ille scribit.*

The master then writes out the whole tense on the board thus:

Ego surgo.   **ego sum magister.**
tu surgis.   **tu es magister.**
ille surgit.   **ille est magister.**
nos surgimus.   **nos sumus magistri.**
vos surgitis.   **vos estis magistri.**
illi surgunt.   **illi sunt magistri.**

As he starts to write, the master addresses the class and says *Scribite,* and all write it out in their exercise books. [It should be explained that each boy has an exercise book in order to write down anything necessary.] Then the master proceeds *Ego sum magister. Quid est hoc?* (taking up the chalk) *Haec est creta.* Then, laying it down and taking it up again, *Quid facio? Cretam capio et scribo.* Then, handing it to a boy, *Cape cretam et scribe "creta." Quid facis?*

P. *Capio cretam.*

M. *Bene. Cretam capis. Quid facit ille?*

Class. *Cretam capit.*

M. *Bene. Cretam capit et scribit. Tu, cape cretam et scribe "capio." Quid facis?*

P. *Capio cretam et scribo.*

M. *Bene. Cretam capis et scribis. Tu, Palinure, cape cretam. Tu es Palinurus. Nomen tibi est Palinurus.* [This was vaguely understood to mean "Your name is Palinurus."] *Quid tibi est nomen?*

P. *Palinurus.*

M. *Dic "nomen mihi est Palinurus."*

P. *Nomen mihi est Palinurus.*

Names were thus given to four or five of the sharper boys, and they were asked in turn *Quid est tibi nomen?* and made to say *Nomen mihi est Urbanus, Viator*, etc. The master then looked round at their writing-out of the present of *surgo* and *sum*, and, finding their English names on their note-books, exclaimed *Quid est hoc? Scribe "Viator," "Urbanus,"* etc., as the case might be. All who had acquired Latin names proceeded to scratch out their English ones and to substitute their newly acquired Latin ones. In naming the boys it is well to keep to real praenomina such as *Marcus, Quintus, Decimus, Sextus, Titus*, etc., or to appropriate renderings of English surnames such as *Faber, Muscus, Lupus*, etc.

For home-work the class was told to learn the two tenses which they had written out.

Next lesson. Revision.

M. *Do tibi cretam. Da mihi cretam. Quid facis?*

P. *Do tibi cretam.*

M. *Quid mihi das?*

P. *Cretam tibi do.*

M. *Bene. Cretam mihi das.* Then, addressing the class but indicating the boy—*Quid facit ille?* and, prompting, *Dat mihi cretam.* Action and question are repeated, and now the class can reply.

Class. *Cretam tibi dat.*

Now the master calls out a boy and, striking him, says *Pulso te. Pulsa me.* As the boy does so the master asks, *Quid facis?*

P. *Pulso te.*

M. *Bene. Pulsas me.* Then to the class, *Ille me pulsat. Quid facit ille?*

Class. *Pulsat te.*

M. *Quem pulsat?*

Class. *Te pulsat.* The order of words is important and should be practised from the beginning, great scope is given for this in the seventh or eighth and, of course, in all subsequent, lessons.

Do, das, dat and *Pulso, pulsas, pulsat* are then revised with different boys.

Then the master places the chalk upon the table, and says *Creta est in mensa; in mensa est creta. Ubi est creta?*

P. *In mensa est creta.*

M. *Bene respondes. Cretam tibi do. Quid facio?*

P. *Cretam mihi das.* This is repeated with different boys. Then the master explains: *In sententia "creta est in mensa," 'creta' est subiectum sententiae, casus est nominativus.*

In sententia "cretam tibi do" 'cretam' est obiectum verbi 'do,' casus est accusativus. Then on the board is written:

Nominativus casus.	CretA	ego	tu
Accusativus casus.	CretAM	me	te
Dativus casus.		mihi	tibi

This is written out by all in their note-books and learnt as home-work. It serves to draw attention to three different cases as such. These particular words are chosen because they have all been correctly *used* and understood by the class already.

This lesson should contain plenty of revision.

Next lesson. Revision.

The master begins by writing on the board:

N.	*CretA*	*UrbanUS*
Acc.	*CretAM*	*UrbanUM*

M. *Urbane, pulsa Palinurum! Quid facis?*

P. *Pulso Palinurus.*

M. *Minime. Pulsas Palinurum.*

This is repeated and the correct answer is obtained.

M. *Palinure, pulsa Urbanum! Quid facis?*

P. *Pulso Urbanum.*

M. *Quid facit Palinurus?*

Class. *Ille pulsat Urbanum.*

This is practised with six or seven pairs of boys. Then the master writes on the board:

A. *Palinurum pulsat Urbanus.*

B. *Urbanum pulsat Palinurus.*

and pointing to (A) asks *Quis pulsat?*

Class. *Urbanus pulsat.*

M. *Bene. Quem pulsat Urbanus?*

Class. *Palinurum pulsat Urbanus.*

The same is done with (B). Similar practice may be made with

A. *Palinurum pulsat Urbanus.*
B. *Palinurus pulsat Urbanum.*

Even the dullest boy cannot help seeing the importance of the endings in such sentences. More names are now given to the boys, and there follows practice of "*Nomen est mihi*," etc. Then a boy is made master, and he practises the "pulsa" business, telling different boys to strike their neighbours, asking each boy what he is doing, and then asking the class what the boy is doing.

The master introduces "*aperio ianuam*" and writes out the present indicative of the four regular conjugations on the board. *Sedeo* had been used already, although the attention of the class had not been drawn to it.

I	II	III	IV
pulso	sedeo	surgo	aperio
pulsas	sedes	surgis	aperis
pulsat	sedet	surgit	aperit
pulsamus	sedemus	surgimus	aperimus
pulsatis	sedetis	surgitis	aperitis
pulsant	sedent	surgunt	aperiunt

This is set to be learnt as home-work.

Next lesson. Practice of the present indicative of the four regular conjugations. Then:

M. *Da mihi cretam. Quid facis?*
P. *Do tibi cretam.*
M. *Urbanum pulsa, Palinure! Quid facis?*
P. *Pulso Urbanum.*
M. *Urbanum quis pulsat?* (to class).

Class. *Palinurus Urbanum pulsat.*
M. *Palinurum pulsa, Urbane! Quid facis?*
P. *Pulso Palinurum.*
M. *Palinurum quis pulsat?*
Class. *Palinurum Urbanus pulsat.*
So with "*Marcum pulsa,*" etc.
M. (touching boy) *Te tango. Quid facio?*
P. *Me tangis.*
M. *Tange Decimum. Quid facis?*
P. *Tango Decimum.*
M. (to class) *Quid facit ille?*
Class. *Ille tangit Decimum.* And so on; then
M. (giving note-book to boy) *Hic est libellus. Libellum tibi do. Quid tibi do?*
P. *Libellum mihi das.*
This is repeated with other boys, then the master gives a pile of note-books to a boy and says: *Tu distribue. Da libellum, et dic "Libellum tibi do; quid facio?"* This boy gives the books round to the whole class and goes through the formula with each boy. The master, addressing this boy upon another boy's reply, says *Dic, "bene," magister!* Thus we get:
Pm. *Libellum tibi do. Quid facio?*
P. *Libellum mihi das.*
Pm. *Bene.*
When a wrong answer came, he was told to say *Male, non bene.*
The master, noticing the absence of a certain boy, says: *Nanus abest. Ubi est Nanus?* As he speaks the master points to the place usually occupied by the boy in question.
M. *Quis abest?*

Class. *Nanus abest.*

M. *Et Dux abest. Nanus et Dux ab*...(pause)

Class. -*sunt.*

Practice follows with other verbs such as *Marcus et Decimus sedent, Quintus et Manlius ambulant*, etc.

Next lesson. Revision.

M. *Abestne Nanus?*

Class. *Non abest.*

M. *Quis abest?* (Prompting) *Nemo abest. Quis abest?*

Class. *Nemo abest.*

M. *Hic est digitus. Quid est?*

Class. *Digitus est.*

M. *Digitum tango. Quid tango?*

Class. *Digitum tangis.*

So with *oculus, nasus, capillus.*

M. *Hic est digitus; magistri est digitus, non est digitus Urbani. Cuius est digitus? Magistri est digitus. Hic est oculus. Magistri est oculus. Cuius est oculus?*

Class. *Magistri est oculus. Cuius* is not, of course, known as the genitive of *quis*, but it is understood, as the answer proves.

M. *Estne hic digitus Urbani?*

Class. *Non, magistri est digitus.*

M. *Capillum Nani tango. Quid tango?*

Class. *Capillum Nani tangis.*

M. *Cuius capillum tango?*

Class. *Nani capillum tangis.* So with *oculus* and *nasus.*

M. *Palinure, tange capillum Bruti. Quid facis?*

P. *Tango capillum Bruti.*

M. *Quid facit Palinurus?*

Class. *Tangit capillum Bruti.*

M. *Cuius capillum tangit?*

Class. *Bruti capillum tangit.*
M. *Hic est nasus; cuius est nasus?*
Class. *Magistri est nasus.*
M. *Estne hic Sexti nasus?*
Class. *Non, Nani est nasus.*
M. *Dicite "Minime; Nani est nasus."*
Class. *Minime; Nani est nasus.*
M. *Da mihi libellum; quid facis?*
P. *Do tibi libellum.*
M. *Cuius est libellus?*
Class. *Decimi est libellus.*
M. *Palinure, libellum Urbani cape et mihi da. Quid facis?*
P. *Libellum Urbani capio et tibi do.*

This is repeated with different boys. The master then writes upon the board:

Nom.	libellus
Voc.	libelle
Acc.	libellum
Gen.	libelli

Next lesson. Revision as usual. Then:

M. Palinure, cape libellum Nani et mihi da. Quid facis?
P. Libellum Nani capio et tibi do.
M. Libellum Nani Urbano da.
P. Libellum Nani Urbano do.
M. Quid facit Palinurus?
Class. Libellum Nani Urbano dat.
M. Decime, cape libellum Sexti et Indico da. Quid facis?
P. Libellum Sexti capio et Indico do.
M. Quid facit Decimus?

Class. Libellum Sexti capit et Indico dat.

M. Quinte, libellum Sexti cape et Sexto da. Quid facis? [*At the moment Indicus, of course, is in possession of the book.*]

P. Libellum Sexti capio et Sexto do.

M. Quid facit Quintus?

Class. Libellum Sexti capit et Sexto dat.

And so on with other boys. Then:

M. (*touching boy's hair*) Quid facio?

Class. Capillum Urbani tangis.

M. Bene. Capillum Urbani digito tango. Quo instrumento capillum Urbani tango? Digito capillum tango. Quo instrumento te tango?

P. Digito me tangis.

M. Digito Nanum tange. Quid facis?

P. Digito Nanum tango.

M. Capillum Quinti digito tange. Quid facis?

P. Capillum Quinti digito tango.

Then "Quid facit ille?" etc.

M. Hic est calamus. Calamo scribimus. Quid facimus calamo?

Class. Scribimus calamo.

M. Quo instrumento scribimus?

Class. Calamo scribimus.

M. Scribite calamo in libellis:

Nom.	libellus
Voc.	libelle
Acc.	libellum
Gen.	libelli
Dat.	libello
Abl.	libello

Next lesson.

M. Te specto. Urbanum specto. Palinurum specto. Quid facio?

Class. Nanum spectas.

M. Sextum digito demonstro. Decimum digito demonstro. Quid facio?

Class. Decimum digito demonstras.

M. Haec est ferula. Hoc est pulpitum. Ferulam capio et pulpitum ascendo. Quid facio?

Class. Ferulam capis et pulpitum ascendas.

M. Male respondetis. Verbum est *ascendo, ascendis, ascendit.* Est tertiae coniugationis. Spectate libellos; primae coniugationis est *pulso,* secundae est *sedeo,* tertiae est *surgo,* quartae est *aperio.* Et *ascendo* simile est verbi *surgo.* Ferulam capio et pulpitum ascendo. Quid facio?

Class. Ferulam capis et pulpitum ascendis.

M. Bene. Nunc, Viator, tu cape ferulam et pulpitum ascende. Quid facis?

P. Capio ferulam et pulpitum ascendo.

M. Ianuam aperio. Quid facio?

Class. Aperis Ianuam.

M. Ianuam claudo. Quid facio?

Class. Ianuam claudis.

M. Tu, Sexte, ianuam claude.

P. Ianuam claudo.

M. (*addressing boy on rostrum*) Tu, Viator, ferula Sextum demonstra, Sextum specta et dic "Ianuam claudis."

P[1]. Ianuam claudis.

M. Tu, Quinte, ferulam cape et pulpitum ascende.

P[2]. Ferulam capio et pulpitum ascendo.

P[1]. Ferulam capis et pulpitum ascendis.

M. Tu, Nane, libellum Decimi cape.

P. Libellum Decimi capio.

P[1]. (*at a nod from the master*) Libellum Decimi capis.

M. (*addressing P*[2]) Tu, Quinte, ferula Nanum demonstra, sed pueros specta, et dic "Libellum Decimi capit."

P[2]. Libellum Decimi capit.

M. Urbane, libellum Palinuri cape et Tauro da.

P. Libellum Palinuri capio et Tauro do.

P[1]. Libellum Palinuri capis et Tauro das.

P[2]. Libellum Palinuri capit et Tauro dat.

So on with other boys and sentences, the two boys on the rostrum always acting as chorus. Then the two chorus-boys are changed thus:

M. Tu, Viator, descende et ferulam Tauro da.

P[1]. Descendo et ferulam Tauro do.

P[2]. Descendit et ferulam Tauro dat.

M. Tu, Taure, ascende.

P. Ascendo.

P[2]. Ascendit.

M. (*addressing P*[2]) Et tu, Quinte, descende et ferulam Decimo da.

P[2]. Descendo et ferulam Decimo do.

The new P[1]. (*at a nod from the master*) Descendis et ferulam Decimo das.

M. Tu, Decime, ascende. [*Decimus is now the new P*[2].]

P[2]. Ascendo.

M. Antoni, libellum Manlio da.

P. Libellum Manlio do.

P[1]. Libellum Manlio das.

P[2]. Libellum Manlio dat.

And so on with other sentences and boys, making frequent changes of chorus-boys.

Next lesson.

At this point it was discovered that the difference between the Subject and Object of a sentence had not been fully grasped by the weaker members of the class, and so for the first quarter of an hour of this lesson a grammatical explanation was given in English of the "Subject-Predicate-Direct Object" *relation, and the difference between such sentences as,*

Palinurus Urbanum pulsat

and, Palinurum Urbanus pulsat

was once more insisted upon. The rest of the lesson was taken up by the writing of words (all so far used) by different boys on the board, in order to make sure that they could correctly write them. Each boy copied down all these words in his note-book. This latter portion of the lesson, was, of course, conducted in Latin.

Next lesson.

It does not seem necessary to give a verbatim report of this and the following lesson. The method is the same as before, e.g.:

M. Hi sunt libelli. Libellos capio. Quid capio?

Class. Libellos capis.

M. Hi sunt oculi. Quid facio (*shutting his eyes*)?

Class. Oculos claudis.

M. Quid nunc facio?

Class. Oculos aperis.

M. Hi sunt pueri. Hi sunt libelli. Libelli puerorum sunt. Quorum sunt libelli?

Class. Puerorum sunt libelli.

M. Puerorum libellos capio. Quid facio?

Class. Puerorum libellos capis.

Plenty of practice. New cases set for home-work.

A thorough revision of last lesson. Then:

M. Hic est liber. Parvus est liber. Hic est liber. Magnus est liber. Qualis est hic liber?

Class. Magnus est liber.

M. Qualis est hic liber?

Class. Parvus est liber.

M. Librum magnum tollo. Quid facio?

Class. Librum magnum tollis.

It should be understood that whenever a mistake is made, as, for example, tollas *here for* tollis, *the master corrects in the manner indicated on p.* 105. *Thus the class becomes familiar with such grammatical terms as* coniugatio *and* declinatio.

M. Librum magni pueri capio et parvo puero do. Quid facio?

Class. Librum magni pueri capis et parvo puero das.

Practise this also with the chorus-boys as on p. 106.

M. Creta est alba. Qualis est creta?

Class. Alba est creta.

M. Estne pulpitum album?

Class. Minime. Creta est alba; pulpitum non est album.

And so on with different coloured books, etc. The singular of parvus *is now written out and learnt as home-work.*

When this point has been reached the first stage in the beginner's course is over. The time has now come for committing to memory the full paradigm of *parvus*, and for abundant practice in the rules of concord. The pupil has *heard* and *spoken*; he must now *see* and *write*. A text-book can be placed in his hands, and he may read simple narrative or dialogue, and work exercises dealing with the text. These should be of two kinds:

(1) Latin questions requiring answers that bring out the chief parts of a sentence, such as, e.g.

[Titus tabulam nigram celeriter purgat]

Quis purgat? Titus purgat.

Quid facit Titus? Purgat Titus.

Quid purgat Titus? Tabulam nigram purgat.

Quomodo purgat Titus tabulam? Celeriter purgat.

It will be seen that the answers to these questions enforce the rules for word-order.

(2) The completion of sentences from which certain endings have been omitted, e.g.

Tit— tabulam nigr— purg—.

English sentences for translation may be set occasionally in order to drive home a new rule or construction, but not before the direct association has been thoroughly established.

The rest of the first year work may be divided into three classes:

(1) The learning of new declensions.

(2) The learning of new tenses, including those of the passive voice.

(3) Practice in the commoner case-usages.

The new declensions do not present any real difficulty. The boys know by this time what a declension means, and no fresh propaedeutic is necessary. If he likes, the teacher can use a few forms, e.g. *pes*, *pedem*, *pedibus*, in conversation before setting the paradigm to be learnt, and to do so certainly strengthens the habit of direct association, but he may find it more convenient for the new paradigm to occur first in the reader. In either case, the declensions will not be given together, or with too short an interval between the old and the new. One fresh declension each week secures a fair rate of progress.

The tenses are a little more troublesome. Oral use should certainly precede the learning of the paradigm and the occurrence of the new forms in the reader. That is to say, the teacher looks out for (or even creates) opportunities of introducing, in a natural and yet striking manner, tense after tense in a convenient sequence. The sequence adopted will depend to a certain extent upon the teacher's own views, but a very useful one is: perfect, future, imperfect, pluperfect, future perfect. One or two examples will make the procedure clear. While a boy is writing on the board the master says *scribis*, and when he has finished writing, *scripsisti*. Two new tenses could be combined into one formula; *scribes* (before the boy writes), *scribis*, *scripsisti*. The boy is made to say on future occasions *scribam*, *scribo*, *scripsi*. For a few days every command to a boy or boys is accompanied by similar drill, and by that time the way for the paradigms has been fully prepared. Suppose a boy confesses ignorance about a point explained the day before. The master's retort might be:

Sed heri exposui; tu tamen ludebas neque animum attendebas.

In this way one use of the imperfect is naturally introduced. The other common use can be brought into a short story beginning, e.g., with:

Olim Romae habitabat senex quidam...

The pluperfect has a natural context in:

Heri iratus eram quia grammaticam non didiceratis.

The future perfect is best reserved until the conjunctions *si* and *cum* require its use.

These examples illustrate the method, but the teacher will ever be ready to seize any occasion that circumstances may afford. Freedom of treatment is essential if the introduction of new forms is to be vitally connected with reality. The later stages in the process of learning—reading, mastery of paradigms, exercises—do not admit of such freedom, and the text-book will be closely, though not slavishly, followed.

The passive voice is best explained by association with actions performed in the class-room. The procedure is essentially the same as that adopted for the active, but, obviously, less time is required. The master may close the door slowly, repeating very deliberately:

Ianua clauditur.

Other sentences will follow:

Picturae moventur,
Creta frangitur,
Ianua panditur.

After a little drill, the agent (*a magistro, a pueris*) can be added, and by this time the class will be ready for the paradigm, many of the brighter members being able to infer by analogy the passive forms of the future and imperfect. The perfect, pluperfect and future perfect passive hardly cause any difficulty, because sentences like *ianua clausa est* are already familiar. The final exercises on the passive should certainly contain many sentences to be changed from the active to the passive, and *vice-versa*.

The verbal forms are so important, and yet so perplexing to a beginner, that special grammatical drill is indispensable. This must be thorough, without being dull or monotonous. In order to avoid wasting time with such long and confusing orders as "Give me the

1st per. pl. of the imperfect indicative passive of *monere*," the writer has devised a series of tables, of which a specimen is here reproduced.

		Praesens	Fut.	Imperf.	Perf.	Plus quam perf.	Fut. et perf.
Sing.	1	XVI	XI	VII	IIII	II	I
	2	XXII	XVII	XII	VIII	V	III
	3	XXVII	XXIII	XVIII	XIII	VIIII	VI
Pl.	1	XXXI	XXVIII	XXIIII	XVIIII	XIIII	X
	2	XXXIIII	XXXII	XXVIIII	XXV	XX	XV
	3	XXXVI	XXXV	XXXIII	XXX	XXVI	XXI

When using the table the master says, e.g., that the voice is active and the verb is *monere*, and then asks for nos.:

XII (monebas)
XX (monueratis)
XXVII (monet)

and so forth. It can all be done in Latin, and an additional interest is added if the boys are made "master" in turn to set questions for their fellows. Surprising as it may seem, these lessons in grammatical accuracy are thoroughly enjoyed by all who take part in them. They arouse as much enthusiasm as a riddle or a puzzle. The teacher should exercise his ingenuity by inventing similar tables for himself. If he writes them out on a large card he will be saved the trouble of continually drawing them on the black-board.

Case-usages will need constant and thorough practice. It is in this department of the work that conversation proves so useful. Every day arises the need to employ the various cases in the course of the class-room routine, and the boys should be encouraged to express themselves in sentences of considerable length, and to avoid single-word answers. It is only a question of training and practice. Diffident at first, in time the boys throw off their shyness and even take a pleasure in volubility. This is a fault on the right side, and to need the rein is a healthier sign than to need the spur. Chance, however, must not be allowed entirely to determine the constructions practised. Knowing the peculiar needs of his class, the teacher can guide the conversation so as to insure drill in the constructions that are least known. If, for example, "agent" and "instrument" are confused, as many sentences as possible will be expressed passively, and the required opportunities for practice will be frequent enough.

A master using the direct method is bound to "take stock" of his class after short intervals. There are at least two definite stages in the process of learning, the stage when the pupil understands but cannot use, and the stage when he both understands and uses. Now the members of even a homogeneous class do not all reach these stages together. Should the teacher be unaware of this he is likely to proceed too quickly, and to leave a majority of the class lagging behind. So periodically—say once every three weeks—he must set a short examination to determine which stage (if either) has been reached. Translation is the most severe test: translation *from* Latin tests the power to understand, translation *into* Latin the power to use. But translation is a test and nothing more. It cannot teach the unknown; so if the results are unsatisfactory the right remedy is, not more translation, but more conversation, more exercises, both oral and written, until translation-tests show that the difficulties have been overcome. It is a great help to tabulate the results of the periodical examinations, and to keep a record of them, so as to know exactly what forms and constructions need attention. Most classes meet their greatest difficulties in the difference between nominative and accusative, the prepositions, and the agreement of adjective and noun, especially when the adjective is of the third declension.

It has recently been maintained[1] that before any passage is read from the reader, not only every construction and new form, but even every new word, ought to be thoroughly mastered in oral practice, so that the reading of a passage is uninterrupted by explanations. This is an ideal which every teacher ought to bear carefully in mind without, however, making a fetish of it or of any other rule. There are reasons why it cannot be adopted without exceptions. Many words are best explained in a written context, not in conversation; a few unknown words add interest to a lesson; finally, the principle of "no interruption" can certainly not be applied to most of Cicero, Virgil and Horace, for the greatest difficulties in the classical writers are rooted in their context and cannot be discussed apart from it.

We will close the chapter on the first year of Latin with an imaginary lesson. It is supposed that towards the end of the second term the passive voice has been begun, but the master discovers that the distinction between "agent" and "instrument" is not understood. Before proceeding with the reader it is necessary that the boys should master the difficulty. One way would be to

[1] By S. O. Andrew in *Praeceptor*.

explain it in English. If, however, Latin be employed, not only is direct association maintained, but a considerable amount of oral practice is secured at the same time.

Master. Tite, Quintum pulsa ferula.
Titus (as he does it) Pulso ferula Quintum.
Master. Pulsatur ferula Quintus. Quintus a Tito ferula pulsatur. "Ferula" sed "a Tito." Cur non "a ferula" et "Tito"?
Boys. Nescimus.
Master. Quia Titus est puer, est homo; vivit et agit; ferula tamen est instrumentum. Non vivit ferula. Nunc respondete. Quo instrumento scribitis?
Boys. Stilo scribimus.
Master. Recte respondetis, quia stilus instrumentum est. Quo instrumento videtis?
Boys. Oculis videmus.
Master. Quis vos docet?
Boys. Tu magister nos doces.
Master. Verte passive, Sexte.
Sextus. A magistro docemur.
Master. Cur "a magistro," Decime?
Decimus. Quia magister est homo; vivit.
Master. A quibus responsa dantur?
Boys. A nobis, a pueris.
Master. Bene. Intellegitisne?
Boys. Intellegimus.

Of course the lesson would not go quite so smoothly as this. Mistakes would occur, and be corrected. But a quarter of an hour is enough to clear away the difficulty and to prepare the class for the section in the reader. This section is here reprinted from the first-year course *Initium*.

Speciēs.

Puer. Quis tū es, speciēs superba?
Speciēs prior. Fōrma quaedam sum verbōrum.
Puer. Et quis tū, speciēs miserābilis?
Speciēs altera. Fōrma quaedam sum verbōrum.
Puer. Sed qūomodo inter vōs discrepātis?
Speciēs I. Ego sum Vōx Āctīva. Āctīva sum quia omnia agō vel faciō—vocō, teneō, claudō, audiō.
Speciēs II. Ego sum Vōx Passīva. Passīva appellor quia nōn agō omnia sed patior—vocor, teneor, claudor, audior. Vōx Āctīva est domina, ego sum serva; illa mē increpat, ego ab illā increpor; illa mē verberat, ego ab illā verberor.
Puer. Altera vestrum est stulta, altera iniūsta. Neutra māiōrem habet potestātem. Utrīque est eadem potestās. Utraque eandem rem sīgnificāre potest. Nihil discrepat inter:

Rōmānī Caesarem necant
et Caesar ā Rōmānīs necātur.

Speciēs I. Nihil discrepat! O scelestum puerum! Verberābō tē!
Speciēs II. Tū ab illā verberāberis.
Speciēs I. Caedam tē!
Speciēs II. Tū ab illā caedēris.
Speciēs I. Poscēs auxilium. Omnēs tē audient.
Speciēs II. Tū ab omnibus audiēris.
Speciēs I. Lacerō tē!
Speciēs II. Ab illā lacerāris.
Puer (*expergīscitur*). Quāle somnium! Nimis herī grammaticae studēbam. Ad multam noctem vigilāvī. Hinc illae speciēs! Nunc surgam, et dum surgō pēnsum iterābō.

Vōx Passīva.

Tempus Praesēns		Tempus Futūrum	
vocor	tangor	vocābor	tangar
vocāris	tangeris	vocāberis	tangēris
vocātur	tangitur	vocābitur	tangētur
vocāmur	tangimur	vocābimur	tangēmur
vocāminī	tangiminī	vocābiminī	tangēminī
vocantur	tanguntur	vocābuntur	tangentur

Tempus Imperfectum	
vocābar	tangēbar
vocābāris	tangēbāris
vocābātur	tangēbātur
vocābāmur	tangēbāmur
vocābāminī	tangēbāminī
vocābantur	tangēbantur

CHAPTER VI

THE NEXT THREE YEARS OF LATIN

§ 1. The Second Year of Latin.

During the first year of Latin nearly all the lessons are of the same type; in the second year they begin to differentiate themselves into two groups, reading lessons and composition lessons, while an occasional period may be devoted to a grammatical point of more than usual difficulty. Every reading period affords much practice in composition, and the time at the teacher's disposal may be divided between the two sorts of lesson in the ratio 4 : 2 or even 5 : 1, without any danger of neglecting composition, either oral or written.

All the work centres round the mastery of the complex sentence in its simpler forms. Certain types have to be learnt in such a way that they can be used accurately and with facility. A book[1] has recently been written in the form of a very simple narrative, the separate sections of which deal with the various types of subordinate clause in turn, many examples of the same type occurring in each section. The mere repetition of examples helps to drive the rule home. A book of this kind is useful, but some teachers hold strongly that when a boy first meets with a new construction a striking appeal should be made to his personal experience. For example, the time has come for (say) final clauses to be learnt. The teacher, on entering the class-room, asks, "Cur adsum? Cur ad vos venio?" One boy is sure to answer, "Venis nos docere." Whereupon the teacher exclaims, "Non ita loquebantur Romani; dic, 'Venis ut nos doceas.'" He follows up this with further examples, and, if they have not been learnt already, the present and imperfect subjunctive of all conjugations are learnt out of the grammar. For some time after this a boy who goes to the black-board to write is made to say "Tabulae appropinquo ut scribam," and this principle of connecting the new construction with actual experience is developed to the utmost. Sometimes quite a long series of sentences, each containing a final clause, is learnt by heart and repeated as a "litany" at the beginning of every lesson for a week.

After this preliminary drill the section on final clauses in some such book as *Pons Tironum* may be read, followed by exercises of a suitable kind, and finally, partly as a test and partly to make yet deeper impressions upon the learner's mind, a set of English sentences may be translated, orally and in writing, into Latin.

It may, and probably will, be wise to give periodically

[1] *Pons Tironum*, by Appleton and Jones.

a lesson, in English, on the new construction. It should come after the preliminary drill and the section in the reader, but before any translation from English into Latin.

Final clauses, of course, are not always expressed in the same way. But the other methods (supine, gerund and *causa*, *qui*, etc.) may all be explained as equivalent to *ut* clauses.

The method of procedure during the second year may best be explained by giving two specimen lessons, one in which reading and practice of a new grammatical point are combined, and one lesson on composition. The former will also afford an opportunity of illustrating the dramatisation of a narrative.

Lesson on a new Grammatical Construction.

Before this lesson is given the master has introduced the class to the construction known as the "dependent command" by giving an order, say *surge*, and then repeating it in the forms *impero tibi ut surgas*, *imperavi tibi ut surgeres*. He has also referred the class to the paradigms of the present and imperfect subjunctive in the grammatical appendix to the reader. The next step is to drive the point home by oral practice before written exercises crown the whole process. The passage here given is about one fourth of the section in *Pons Tironum* which deals with this particular construction (p. viiii).

Ante lucem servus quidam nomine Davus ad cellam, ubi dormio, venit; fores pulsat, ac mihi ut surgam imperat. Ego dormire volo; servo igitur ut abeat impero. Servus abit, sed pater eum redire iubet. Redit igitur et clamans "Pater tuus," inquit, "ut statim surgas tibi imperat." E lectulo, in quo dormiebam, sine mora surgo; sed vestes, quibus me induere soleo, invenire non possum. Davo igitur ut novam tunicam quaerat impero. Ille autem "Cur," inquit, "quod mater tibi imperat numquam facis? Cur ei non pares? Nam semper tibi imperat ut tunicam apud lectulum tuum deponas." Ego tamen iratus ei ut taceat impero. Tacet igitur et alii imperat servo ut tunicam novam mihi det. Servus ille alteram tunicam adfert, et mihi "Davus," inquit, "ut hanc tunicam tibi darem mihi imperavit. Imperavit quoque ut celeriter te vestires."

Magister. Salvete, discipuli. Spectate nonam paginam. Quid vobis impero, Quinte?

Quintus. Magister, ut nonam paginam spectamus imperas.

Magister. Male. Quis potest emendare sententiam?

Titus. Imperas nobis ut nonam paginam spectemus.

Magister. Recte emendavisti, Tite. Sed quid imperavi? Tu responde, Sexte.

Sextus. Ut nonam spectaremus paginam imperavisti.

Magister. Bene, immo vero optime. Nunc recita primam sententiam. Impero tibi ut recites.
[Sextus recitat.]

Magister. Quis quid ignorat?

Quintus. Quid significat "cella"?

Magister. O puerorum omnium stultissimum! Sententia ipsa declarat. Quis potest Quintum adiuvare?

Decimus. Locus ubi dormio, conclave.

Magister. Recte respondes. Quid aliud ignoratis?

Titus. "Fores."

Magister. Inspicite omnes indicem verborum, et tu, Tite, recita.

Titus (recitans). Fores, -um, feminini generis; ianua quae duas habet partes; aliter *valvae.*

Magister. Intellegitisne?
Omnes. Ita.
Magister. Surge, Flacce. Recita duas sententias.
[Flaccus recitat.]
Magister. Num omnia sunt clara?
Titus. Minime. Quid significat "iubet"?
Magister. Idem quod "imperat." Sed observate constructionem. "Iubet eum redire," hoc est, "imperat ei ut redeat." Iubeo te, Tite, scribere in tabula huius verbi partes:—
iubeo, iubere, iussi, iussum.
[Titus scribit.]
Nunc iubeo omnes in libellis scribere.
[Omnes scribunt.]
Quid iussi? Universi respondete.
Omnes. Scribere nos iussisti.
Magister. Perge, Flacce. Recita tres sententias.
[Flaccus recitat.]
Quintus. Ignoro "induere."
Magister. Cogita, Quinte. Iubeo te cogitare. Impero tibi ut cogites. "Induere me vestibus soleo."
Quintus. Intellego, sed aliter exponere non possum.
Magister. Inspice igitur indicem verborum. Quid illic vides?
Quintus (recitans). Induo, -ere, -ui, -utum; fere idem quod *vestio*. Induo me *vel* induo vestem.
Magister. Discite partes. Recita, Rex, tres sententias.
Rex. Sed quid est "tunica"?
Magister. Index declarabit. Inspice indicem et recita.
Rex (recitans). Tunica, -ae, feminini generis; vestis quae sub ceteris est vestibus.
Magister. Spectate picturam. Haec est tunica. Nunc recita, Rex.

[Rex recitat.]

Rex. "Pares" non intellego.

Magister. Heu! In indice non inest. Oportet igitur vos scribere. Pareo, parere, parui.
Dicimus "pareo alicui" non "aliquem," et significat idem quod "oboedio."

Rex. Sed quid significat "oboedio"?

Magister. Si facis id quod iubeo, mihi oboedis vel pares. Scribite omnes. Tu, Quinte, recita usque ad finem.
[Quintus recitat.]
Quid non clarum est?

Omnes. Nihil.

Magister. Bene. Nunc spectate exercitationes.

The *exercitationes* are questions of these types:

(I) Adde partes vocabulorum omissas:

1. Servus mihi imperat ut surg—
2. Servus mihi imperat ut tunicam quaer—
3. Pater filio imperat ut tac—
4. Pater filio imperav— ut tac—

etc.

(II)

1. Quid mihi imperat servus?
2. Quid servo impero?
3. Quid semper imperat mihi mater?
4. Quid imperavit mihi Davus?

etc.

These present little or no difficulty, but are worked through rapidly *viva voce*, and, if there is time, in writing.

The next lesson continues the work of the one preceding it, or, if the master thinks that the construction is well understood, he may use the recently acquired material for a composition lesson. The first step is to have the whole passage from *Ante lucem* to *vestires* read over by one or possibly two boys. Then books are shut and the boys try to repeat the narrative sentence by sentence, the master suggesting the sequence of ideas when everybody is at a loss. When the whole is finished orally, it is perhaps written out, without book, in order to close the lesson. Perhaps, however, the master prefers to substitute for the written exercise a rough dramatisation of the narrative. One boy becomes Lucius, another Davus, another the second slave, Phormio. Then, with books open, the boys and master together work out the following dialogue:

Davus. Surge, Luci. Iubeo te surgere.
Lucius. Aliquis fores pulsat. Quis adest?
Davus. Davus adsum. Imperabam tibi ut surgeres.
Lucius. Sed nolo surgere; dormire volo. Abi, Dave. [Davus abit et cito redit.]
Davus. Pater tuus te sine mora surgere iubet.
Lucius. Dave, vestes invenire non possum. Quaere mihi alteram tunicam.
Davus. Cur matri non oboedis? Semper enim te iubet tunicam prope lectulum tuum deponere.
Lucius (iratus). Tace, tace, pessime. Abi et adfer tunicam.
Phormio. Davus mihi imperavit ut tunicam tibi adferrem. Haec est. Davus redire nonvolt quia tu iratus es. Imperavit quoque ut celeriter te vestires.

Other boys now take the three parts, and this time a few additions or alterations may be tried, or an attempt may be made to go through the piece without books. A suitable task for home-work would be to write the dialogue from memory, without reference to the narrative in the text-book.

Lesson on Composition.

We now give a specimen of a narrative told by the master to be reproduced by the boys.

Magister. Olim seni cuidam Romano erat psittacus, qui—.

Pueri nonnulli. Psittacus? Quid "psittacus"?

Magister. Avis est. Ego scribo nomen.

Quintus. Nonne viridis est?

Magister. Ita; et humana voce loquitur.

Omnes (subridentes). Intellegimus.

Magister. Psittacus ille in cavea habitabat, ex qua se liberare cupiebat. Nunc tu quoque, Tite, dic sententiam.

Titus. Olim seni cuidam Romano erat psittacus qui caveam aegre ferens se liberare cupiebat.

Magister. Nunc universi dicite.
[Omnes dicunt.]
Itaque huiusmodi consilium iniit.

Sextus. Iniit?

Magister. Ita. A verbo "inire" est ductum. "Inire consilium" est "consilium capere." Universi dicite. [Omnes dicunt.] Mane dominus, ad caveam progressus ut cibum et aquam renovaret, psittacum vidit in ima cavea iacentem, alis extentis pedibusque ad caelum erectis.

Decimus. Alis?

Magister. "Ala" est avis membrum. Instrumentum est quo usa volat.

Decimus. Intellego.

Rex. Scribe, magister, partes verborum "iacentem," "extentis," "erectis." Ego obliviscor.

Magister. Oblitus es, Rex. Ego scribam. [Scribit.]

Quintus. Num psittacus mortus erat?

Magister. Festina lente, Quinte. Statim disces. Sed quid istud "mortus"? Corrige, Sexte.

Sextus. Mortuus.

Magister. Recte. Nunc ad rem redeamus. Quis sententiam dicere potest?

Vergilius. Ego possum. Mane senex ad caveam ivit et vidit psittacum alas extendentem.

Magister. Non ita male narravisti. Sed melius est "progressus vidit" quam "ivit et vidit," et "alis extentis" quam "alas extendentem."

Vergilius. Cur?

Magister. Quia psittacus erat quietus. Non extendebat alas; alae iam erant extentae. Nunc pergo. "O me miserum," inquit senex, "psittacus meus est mortuus." Quibus dictis ianuam caveae pandit et inserta manu psittacum extrahit. Tu dic, Sexte. [Sextus dicit.] Nunc universi dicite. [Omnes dicunt.] Deinde senex corpus psittaci in hortum ut sepeliret extulit; quo facto in villam rursus intravit ut ligonem adferret.

Titus. Quid est "ligonem"?

Magister. Ligo, ligonis, masculini generis. Scribe, Tite. Instrumentum est quo terram fodimus. Nunc, Quinte, velim totam narres fabulam ab initio usque ad finem. [Quintus narrat. Magister corrigit corrigenda.] Nunc ego pergam. Foras egressus psittacum videt nullum, sed vox ex arbore vicina sonat: "Non omnia sunt talia qualia videntur esse." Dic, Sexte. [Sextus dicit.] Quis potest totam fabulam emendate narrare?

Titus. Ego conabor, magister. [Narrat.]

Magister. Bene. Nunc omnes scribite.

If necessary, the writing out of the story may be reserved for home-work.

§ 2. THE THIRD AND FOURTH YEARS OF LATIN.

During these years the method of working is much the same as the one employed in the second, but the programme is more ambitious. The boys know more; their minds have developed, and they are prepared to exchange the trifles of the first two years for a more severe study of the classics themselves. The periods of work may be divided as follows:

Reading	3 to 5 per week
Composition (including dramatisation, etc.)	2 per week
Special grammar lessons and, during the fourth year only, unseens	1 per week

A knowledge of the outlines of Roman history is necessary at this stage, and unless a place can be found for the subject elsewhere, some elementary text-book must be studied as home-work. The fourth year composition includes Latin proses of the ordinary type, and in that year one period every fortnight is reserved for an "unseen." The regular grammar is finished during the third year, and the grammar lessons of the fourth year include a short course in comparative idiom, special attention being paid to the common types of period. This course will serve to some extent as a series of demonstrations in translation, and occasionally, perhaps once a fortnight, the reader should be translated instead of read. An excellent, perhaps the best, form of home-work is an English rendering of the Latin paraphrased in school.

Caesar is not a good author for these years. Appealing to mature minds this writer should be reserved for private reading in the sixth. But a part of some book, for example the attack on Cicero's camp—a miniature prose epic—may well be read towards the close of the third year. During this year one book of Virgil should be read; boys love the Taking of Troy. A few of the easiest odes of Horace, and some selections from Livy, simplified if necessary, will fully occupy the time at our disposal.

The fourth year needs very careful thought. Many boys will probably finish their Latin course at the end of it, and it is important that they should not miss what is best in Latin literature. Perhaps the most suitable selection would be Cicero *de senectute* and *pro Archia*, the sixth *Aeneid*, Tacitus *Agricola* and the finest stories from Ovid. Some passages, after careful preparation in class and translation at home, should certainly be learnt by heart.

Composition, translation, grammar and unseens are dealt with elsewhere. The reading lessons for both years are of the same type, but they gradually increase in freedom of treatment as time goes on and a greater command of the language is acquired. There are paraphrases of difficulties, written in note-books and learnt at home, questions and answers in Latin, summaries in Latin and occasional dramatisation of suitable passages.

One word in conclusion. All lessons in which Latin only is spoken are *ipso facto* composition lessons. More power of expression is acquired on the direct method than in any other way.

CHAPTER VII

THE FIRST TWO YEARS OF GREEK

It is a sound principle that two new languages should never be begun at the same time, and the study of Greek is better postponed until Latin has been learnt for two years at least. The beginner accordingly will be about fourteen years old. His first task will be to master the new script and practise the new pronunciation. The former is always a source of great pleasure, partly because of the novelty, but also because the Greek letters are beautiful. Pronunciation, always an object of care to "direct" teachers, is especially so in the case of Greek, and the general phonetics of the pre-classical course prove most useful. The sounds corresponding to the vowel-letters and their combinations are roughly those recommended by the Classical Association. The vowels are kept pure; iota subscript is pronounced (ῳ like οι with the first component lengthened), and η is carefully distinguished from ει.

Quantity is fastidiously observed, and the boys are prevented from showing quantity by mere stress—a common blunder in English mouths.

In one school at least a serious attempt is made to pronounce the accents. The acute is a rising tone, the circumflex a rising-falling tone, and the second accent in *τὸν ἄνδρα* is a fraction of a tone higher than the first. Careful attention to pronunciation, quantity and accent makes the reading of Greek a real pleasure; one realises, however imperfectly, the rich melody of the language. The time spent upon the task is insignificant when compared with the advantages to be gained from correct and fluent speech.

After two years of Latin a boy is familiar with a number of grammatical forms, and with the general grammatical scheme of a language very near akin to Greek. This fact will affect method in so far as there is no need to repeat propaedeutic exercises which before were indispensable. Accordingly, progress is twice as rapid, for not only is linguistic experience greater, but in the two years' interval the mind has grown and developed. But in no way is the principle altered that directness of association takes precedence of most other considerations. A few expressions, in fact most conjunctions and prepositions, are best explained by English equivalents. It would be a sin to fall down and worship any method, under the impression that the slightest deviation from it is heresy. But surprisingly little English is actually necessary, even at the first, and a conscientious master will remember that the more English is used, the more it tends to be used, because it appears to save trouble. It is often possible to concentrate the English explanations into one lesson occurring periodically, so as to avoid the repeated mental dislocations of a "mixed" lesson.

As was the case in the Latin lessons, the master must not be discouraged by the number of small errors which are sure to occur. Fluency is almost necessarily accompanied by mistakes at first. If the general sense is understood, if the details become clearer as time goes on, and if mistakes are corrected in the oral stage before writing has impressed them upon the mind, little or no harm will be done. As the focussing of a telescope alters blurred to distinct vision, so will time, practice, and criticism change correct vagueness to correct accuracy. Too much attention to details at first causes in many cases an incurable indifference to idiom and sense.

The text-books used are, for the first year, a Greek grammar and Rouse's *Greek Boy at Home*, and, for the second year, the same grammar and a selection from the following classical authors or works:

Lucian: *Dialogues of the Dead.*

Plato: *Ion, Crito, Euthyphro, Apology.*

Thucydides: some dramatic episode like Pylos and Sphacteria, the Siege of Plataea or the Sicilian Expedition.

Herodotus: selections.

Homer: two books.

Herodotus makes an admirable reader for the second year, except that the dialect is a little confusing. An atticised Herodotus at this stage would be a great boon. Homer presents less difficulty than might have been expected. His peculiarities are accepted as being "poetical," and the strange forms are paraphrased by Attic equivalents.

No composition book is used, as practically all the composition done is reproduction of one type or another. The few pieces of translation which are set as a test of progress may very well be dictated by the master and based upon the reader.

Six periods a week are required, and during the first two terms they will be undifferentiated (reading, grammar and composition being combined) unless the master think fit to begin reproduction during the second term. During the remaining four terms four lessons may be devoted to reading and two to composition. Grammar can be taken during the first ten minutes of the reading lessons. Dramatisation, of course, will be one form of composition employed. Translation into English is used mainly as a test. The greater part of the accidence and the commoner forms of the complex sentence can easily be worked through during the first year, the pace being twice as fast as it was with Latin.

Two experiments have been tried in the treatment of the lessons immediately following the learning of the alphabet. The teacher may begin with a few paradigms, *καλός, καλή, καλόν*, the article and the present indicative, and use these as a basis for conversation, and for discussion of the first page or so of the reader. On the other hand he may model the first Greek lessons very closely on those adopted for Latin, and associate *γράφω, γράφεις, τράπεζα, θύρα, διδάσκαλος, παιδίον*, and so forth, with the routine of the class-room. The reader will be attacked as soon as some facility in very easy sentences has been acquired. It is somewhat difficult to compare results, but it seems to be true that progress is more rapid on the former method during the first fortnight, but on the latter the preliminary drill in direct association brings a surer and quicker advance later on.

We will now pass on to the time when the reader is begun. A paragraph is read out sentence by sentence. After each sentence there is a pause during which the master explains anything that is not understood. This explanation will be very slow and laborious at first if English be excluded, but perseverance will soon bring a rich reward in increased speed and greater interest. The paraphrases are generally written on the black-board and copied into note-books, to be learnt by heart as part of the home-work. Paradigms are declined or conjugated, and questions are asked (in Greek) on the text. These at first are of the simplest kind, being designed to bring out the main parts of each sentence. For example:

ὁ πατήρ μου οἰκίαν ἔχει ἐν ἀγροῖς.
Q. *τίς οἰκίαν ἔχει;* A. *ὁ πατήρ μου ἔχει οἰκίαν.*
Q. *τί ἔχει ὁ πατήρ σου;*
A. *οἰκίαν ἔχει ὁ πατήρ μου.*
Q. *ποῦ ἐστιν ἡ οἰκία τοῦ σοῦ πατρός;*
A. *ἐν ἀγροῖς ἐστιν ἡ οἰκία τοῦ ἐμοῦ πατρός.*

The answers are given first with books open and then with books shut. Sometimes they are finally written.

Gradually the questions are made more difficult, and in time continuous reproduction is introduced. After six weeks' work the class ought to be "getting into their stride," and able to compose accurately very simple sentences with a limited vocabulary. Progress from this point onwards ought to be both sure and rapid, especially as a Greek set usually consists of bright boys.

A specimen lesson is now given from the Board of Education pamphlet, *The Teaching of Greek at the Perse School.* It is taken from the work of the second term.

Boys: Γλαῦκος, Κλέαρχος, Ὅμηρος, Αἰσχύλος, Εὐριπίδης, Σωκράτης.

Home-work: To learn *γένος* and *πόλις*, and to prepare 10 lines of the reader which have been partly explained by Greek paraphrase beforehand.

Διδάσκαλος. *χαίρετε, ὦ μαθηταί.*
Μαθηταί. *χαῖρε, ὦ διδάσκαλε.*
Δ. *Μὴ προσβλέπετε τὸ βιβλίον, κελεύω ὑμᾶς μὴ προσβλέπειν τὸ βιβλίον. ὦ Σώκρατες, τί κελεύω;*

Σ. Κελεύεις ἡμᾶς μὴ προσβλέπειν τὸ βιβλίον.
Δ. Ὀρθῶς ἀποκρίνει· τί ἐκέλευσα, ὦ Γλαῦκε;
Γ. Ἐκέλευσας ἡμᾶς μὴ προσβλέπειν τὸ βιβλίον.
Δ. Καὶ σύ, ὦ Γλαῦκε, ὀρθῶς λέγεις. τί ποιεῖτε;
Μ. Οὐ προσβλέπομεν τὸ βιβλίον.
Δ. Ἀρχώμεθα ἄρα· μανθάνωμεν τὴν γραμματικήν. ἐγὼ μὲν οὖν ἄρχομαι, "ἡ πόλις"· σὺ δὲ πρόιθι, ὦ Κλέαρχε.
Κ. Ἀλλά, ὦ διδάσκαλε, οὐ μανθάνω τὸ πρόιθι.
Δ. Τὸ πρόιθι τὸ αὐτὸ νοεῖ τῷ πρόβαινε.
Κ. Ἀλλ' οὐδὲ τὸ πρόβαινε μανθάνω.
Δ. Οἴμοι τῆς σῆς ἀμαθίας, οἴμοι τῆς ἀμαθίας σου· ἀμφοτέρως ἀποκρίνου, ὦ Γλαῦκε.
Γ. Οἴμοι τῆς [1]μῆς ἀμαθίας—
Δ. Ἁμαρτάνεις· τί ἔδει λέγειν, ὦ Ὅμηρε;
Ο. Τῆς ἐμῆς ἀμαθίας.
Γ. Οἴμοι τῆς ἐμῆς ἀμαθίας, οἴμοι τῆς ἀμαθίας μου.

[The master now explains that πρόιθι is the imperative of πρόειμι, I go on, and the imperative and present indicative of εἶμι are learnt from the grammar.]

Δ. Λαβὲ νῦν τὴν γύψον, καὶ γράψον τὸ πρόιθι.
[ὁ Γλαῦκος γράφει τὸ προίθι.]
Οἴμοι μάλ' αὖθις· οὐ γὰρ ὀρθῶς ἔγραψας τὸν τόνον. γράψον τὸ πρόιθι. ἆρα ὀρθῶς ἔγραψεν, ὦ μαθηταί;
Μ. Ὀρθῶς.
Δ. Νῦν ἀρχώμεθα πάλιν ἀπ' ἀρχῆς. λέγε, ὦ Γλαῦκε, "ἡ πόλις."
Γ. Ἡ πόλις, ὦ πόλι, τὴν πόλιν κ.τ.λ.
Δ. Ὀρθῶς. σύ, ὦ Αἰσχύλε, λέγε "τὸ γένος."
[Ὁ Αἰσχύλος ὀρθῶς λέγει.]
Νῦν γράφετε πάντες τὰ ὀνόματα ταῦτα. τί κελεύω;
Μ. Κελεύεις ἡμᾶς πάντας γράφειν τὰ ὀνόματα.
[Γράφουσι, καὶ γραφόντων αὐτῶν περιπατεῖ ὁ διδάσκαλος καὶ μεταγράφει τὰς ἁμαρτίας.]

[1] Mistakes of this kind are, of course, fairly common during the earlier lessons. They must be carefully corrected, and the pupil should repeat the correct answer at least once.

Δ. Νῦν ἀναγιγνώσκωμεν τὸν μῦθον τὸν περὶ τοῦ ψιττακοῦ. ἀλλὰ μὴν ἐγὼ ἤδη κάμνω—ἆρα μανθάνετε ὅ τι σημαίνει τὸ κάμνω;

Μ. Οὐ μανθάνομεν.

[The verb is explained by action or in English (not translated by a word, but paraphrased) and the chief parts learnt.]

Δ. Ἐμοῦ κάμνοντος, σύ, ὦ Εὐριπίδη, ἴσθι διδάσκαλος. ταχέως οὖν ἀνάβαινε ἐπὶ τὸ βῆμα καὶ δίδασκε. ἀγαθὸς γὰρ εἶ διδάσκαλος, ἄριστος μὲν οὖν.

[Ὁ Εὐριπίδης ἀναβαίνει καὶ καθίζει.]

Ε. Ὁρᾶτε πάντες τὴν δέλτον τὴν ὀγδόην καὶ τὸν πρῶτον στίχον. πόστην δέλτον, ὦ Γλαῦκε;

Γ. Τὴν ὀγδόαν δέλτον.

Δ. (ὑπολαβών) Μὴ λέγε ὀγδόαν, ἀλλὰ ὀγδόην· ὄγδοος, ὀγδόη, ὄγδοον. καὶ σύ, ὦ Αἰσχύλε, μὴ παῖζε. τί κελεύω, ὦ Εὐριπίδη;

Ε. Κελεύεις τὸν Αἰσχύλον μὴ παίζειν.

Δ. Λέγετε ταῦτα πάντες.

[Λέγουσι.]

Πρόιθι, ὦ Εὐριπίδη.

Ε. Ἄρχου ἀναγιγνώσκειν Ἑλληνιστί, ὦ Αἰσχύλε.

[Ἀναγιγνώσκει ὁ Αἰσχύλος περὶ τοῦ ψιττακοῦ στίχους ἑπτά.]

Παῦε, ὦ Αἰσχύλε.

Α. Παύομαι.

Ε. Κάθιζε, καὶ ὑμεῖς οἱ ἄλλοι μὴ προσβλέπετε τὸ βιβλίον. τίς οἷός τέ ἐστι λέγειν ἄνευ βιβλίου τὸ πρῶτον μέρος τοῦ μύθου;

Α. Ἀλλὰ τί νοεῖ τὸ μέρος; οὐ μανθάνω ἔγωγε.

Δ. Ἐγὼ ἀποκρινοῦμαι ἀντὶ σοῦ, ὦ Εὐριπίδη· μέρος δύναται μόριον, Ἀγγλιστὶ "part." τὸ μέρος, τοῦ μέρους, τῷ μέρει, καὶ τὰ λοιπά, ἀτεχνῶς ὥσπερ τὸ γένος, ὃ νῦν δὴ ἐμάθετε. πρόιθι, ὦ Εὐριπίδη.

Ε. Τίς οἷός τέ ἐστι λέγειν;

Γ. Ἐγὼ οἷός τέ εἰμι.

ὄρνιθ' ἔχω κατ' οἶκον,
ὃς ψιττακὸς καλεῖται.

κάλλιστός ἐστιν ὄρνις,
καὶ ποικίλος τὸ χρῶμα.
καὶ θαῦμα δὴ μέγιστον·
ὅταν γὰρ οἴκαδ' ἔλθω,
"ὦ χαῖρέ" φησ' "ἄριστε."

E. Ἑρμήνευε Ἀγγλιστί.

A translation of the piece is then given.

As soon as fair fluency has been gained there should follow plenty of reading. This ought to err on the side of easiness rather than that of difficulty, so as to insure an increasing vocabulary and continuous practice in common constructions. Our object is not to provide a series of linguistic puzzles, but to secure a command of normal idiom. The reading should be diversified with reproduction, either of sections of the reader or of narratives read by the teacher. The latter best preserve the psychological order—*hear, speak, write.* A reproduction lesson for the second year is now given[1]; it is so simple that it would not be above the heads of a good first-year class in the third term.

Διδάσκαλος. Ἀκούετε πάντες. μῦθον γάρ τινα μέλλω ὑμῖν λέγειν. ἦν ποτε φιλόσοφός τις Ἀθηναῖος, ὀνόματι Κλεάνθης. γράφε, ὦ Αἰσχύλε, τὸ ὄνομα εἰς τὴν σανίδα· εὖγε. ὁ δὲ τὴν μὲν σοφίαν πάνυ ἐφίλει, χρήματα δὲ οὐκ εἶχε· πένης γὰρ ἦν. ἤθελε μὲν οὖν Ζήνωνος ἀκροᾶσθαι, φιλοσόφου τινὸς ἀρίστου καὶ ἐνδοξοτάτου.

Εὐριπίδης. Οὐ συνίημι τὸ ἀκροᾶσθαι.

Διδάσκαλος. Μαθητὴν εἶναί τινος, ἢ ἀκούειν διδασκάλου. καὶ οἱ Ἕλληνες ἔλεγον ἀκροᾶσθαί τινος οὐκ ἀκροᾶσθαί τινα. οὕτως οὖν πένης ἦν ὥστε οὐκ ἐδύνατο (μὴ δύνασθαι). ὦ Κλέαρχε, αὖθις λέγε ἃ ἔλεγον.

Κλέαρχος. Κλεάνθης, φιλόσοφός τις ὤν, οὕτω πένης ἦν ὥστε Ζήνωνος μαθητὴς γίγνεσθαι οὐκ ἐδύνατο.

[1] From the Board of Education *Report on the Teaching of Greek at the Perse School.*

Διδάσκαλος. Ὀρθῶς. νῦν λέγετε σύμπαντες. [λέγουσι.] νυκτὸς οὖν ἐν τοῖς κήποις ἀνδρὸς πλουσίου ὕδωρ ἤντλει.

Ὅμηρος. Τί νοεῖ τὸ κήποις καὶ τὸ ἤντλει;

Διδάσκαλος. Κῆπός ἐστι τόπος ἐν ᾧ φύεται δένδρα τε καὶ φυτὰ ἄλλα.

Ὅμηρος. Ἆρα νοεῖ ὅπερ ἐκάλουν οἱ Ῥωμαῖοι "*hortus*";

Διδάσκαλος. Οὕτως. καὶ ἀντλῶ (ὥσπερ τὸ ποιῶ) ὕδωρ ἐκ τῆς γῆς μηχανῇ τινι χρώμενος. νῦν προΐωμεν. νυκτὸς μὲν οὖν ἤντλει ὁ Κλεάνθης, ἡμέρας δὲ ἐφιλοσόφει παρὰ τῷ Ζήνωνι. γράφε, ὦ Ὅμηρε, τὸ ἀντλῶ. ὁρῶντες δὲ οἱ Ἀθηναῖοι ὅτι πένης ὢν φιλοσοφεῖ καὶ οὐ χρηματίζεται ἀλλὰ τοῦ χρηματισμοῦ ἀμελεῖ, εἰσάγουσι παρὰ τοὺς δικαστάς. ἐρωτώμενος δὲ ὁπόθεν ἔχει τὴν τροφὴν πάντα ἐδήλωσε τὰ γιγνόμενα. τίς τί ἀγνοεῖ;

Αἰσχύλος. Ἀγνοῶ τὸ χρηματίζομαι.

Διδάσκαλος. Χρήματα ἐμαυτῷ πορίζομαι, ἐπὶ μισθῷ ἐργάζομαι, μισθὸν λαμβάνω. γράφε ταῦτα πάντα. νῦν προΐωμεν. ἀκούσαντες δὲ οἱ δικασταὶ πάνυ ἐθαύμαζον αὐτὸν τῆς φιλοπονίας καὶ δέκα μνᾶς δοθῆναι αὐτῷ ἐψηφίσαντο.

Ὅμηρος. Διὰ τί τὸ τῆς φιλοπονίας;

Διδάσκαλος. Ὥσπερ λέγεις καὶ τὸ οἴμοι τῆς λήθης μου καὶ τὰ λοιπά. νῦν ἐρωτήσω ὑμᾶς οὐ πολλά. τίς ἦν ὁ Κλεάνθης;

Πάντες. Φιλόσοφος ἦν.

Διδάσκαλος. Καὶ ὁ Ζήνων;

Πάντες. Φιλόσοφος ἦν καὶ οὗτος.

Διδάσκαλος. Ποῖος δέ τις ἦν ὁ Κλεάνθης; σὺ ἀποκρίνου, ὦ Κλέαρχε.

Κλέαρχος. Πένης ἦν, καὶ φιλοσοφεῖν οὐκ ἐδύνατο.

Διδάσκαλος. Τί ἄρα ἐποίησεν;

Κλέαρχος. Νυκτὸς μὲν ἤντλει παρὰ πλουσίῳ τινὶ ἐν κήποις, ἡμέρας δὲ τοῦ Ζήνωνος ἠκροᾶτο.

Διδάσκαλος. Καὶ τί ἐποίησαν οἱ Ἀθηναῖοι νομίζοντες αὐτὸν κλέπτην εἶναι;

Αἰσχύλος. Ἆρα οὕτως ἐνόμιζον;

Διδάσκαλος. Οὕτως· πένης γὰρ ὢν ἐφιλοσόφει χρήματα τῷ Ζήνωνι δούς.

Αἰσχύλος. Μανθάνω. εἰσήγαγον αὐτὸν παρὰ τοὺς δικαστάς.

Διδάσκαλος. Πρόιθι, ὦ Ὅμηρε.

Ὅμηρος. Πάντα δὲ ἀκούσαντες ἀπέγνωσαν αὐτὸν τῆς γραφῆς δέκα μνᾶς δοθῆναι ψηφιζόμενοι.

Διδάσκαλος. Νῦν γράφετε πάντες τὸν μῦθον.

CHAPTER VIII

THE SIXTH FORM AND AFTER

For thirteen years the writer has taught, not in different years but at different hours of the day for the whole period, pupils at every stage from *mensa* to the tripos. For some of these he has been responsible during the whole of their course. He can therefore fairly claim not only to be in a position to compare the results of the direct method with those of the other, but also to offer some advice to those who are engaged in teaching older scholars. First let us consider a few general points.

There is certainly room for more organisation in many branches of the work. Much is left to chance and haphazard which ought to be reduced to system. The acquirement of a working vocabulary is rarely planned in an orderly manner, and yet its importance can scarcely be exaggerated. Each student ought to make vocabularies for himself. A large exercise-book can be divided into sections with subject headings, about twenty in all, such as politics, warfare, farming and the country, religion, morality, home-life, law, food, clothing and so forth. One section, and that a large one, is reserved for unclassified words and idioms. Into this book the student enters, as he comes across them in the course of his reading, phrases which strike him as likely to prove useful in composition. He may add references, and some mark to signify whether the expression is peculiar to prose or verse, or, in the case of Greek, to some particular dialect. He will soon have at his disposal a true *vade mecum*, a book constantly at his side when he is composing. He must make a special point of using at the earliest opportunity each new phrase he registers, for once used it will be a more permanent possession, lingering at the back of his mind and ready to rush to the foreground of consciousness whenever occasion calls for it.

A similar method ought to be adopted in the case of sentence-structure. The different types of the sentence and of the period are not very numerous, and can easily be ascertained by spending a few days in the analysis of interesting passages from Thucydides, Sophocles, Cicero and Virgil. These types, when discovered, should be entered into a dozen pages or so at the beginning or end of the vocabulary-book. Stress must again be laid upon the necessity of using the knowledge so acquired, in order that it may become part of the pupil's mental stock-in-trade. He should say to himself: "During the next week I will try to use *ita...ut*, or a stressed Greek participle," or, "I will try to write a complex sentence with the relative placed before its antecedent." One of the great advantages of free composition at the advanced stage is that the master can set a theme on a given subject and require certain constructions to occur in it, thus securing in time practice in all the important types.

The learning of particles should surely not be left to chance. Paley's little book is good, but a classified collection made by the student himself is much better. They should be divided into three kinds:

(1) those which connect;

(2) those which anticipate another particle;

(3) those which make prominent a word or a phrase, or give a sort of "flavour" to the whole sentence.

Enclitics, of course, should be distinguished in some way from the rest. One of the commonest mistakes is to suppose that any particle may connect one sentence with the preceding. The plan here recommended prevents this mistake. Combinations of particles must be included in the list, and examples from authors read in class or privately are indispensable.

All this tabulation of facts will need the careful supervision of the teacher. His part is to outline a general scheme, to suggest illuminating quotations, to inspect periodically the progress of the work and to be ready with improvements. In all his private work, and this naturally increases in amount as time goes on, the student ought to feel the guiding hand of his teacher. Independent effort flourishes best when aided by sympathy, stimulus and inspiration.

The reading list is often filled up in a haphazard fashion which has a prejudicial effect upon progress. Surely it were better to attack subjects in turn—epic, history, drama, oratory and philosophy—and to group the reading of authors round these. A thorough carrying out of this plan involves considerable difficulties in staffing and organisation, but a modification of it has been for some years in vogue at Newnham College, Cambridge, with excellent results.

During the last generation so much progress has been made in certain branches of classical study, especially in history and archaeology, that there is some danger lest the student sacrifice thoroughness and accuracy in the endeavour to amass information. The danger may be met by making an effort to acquire the necessary knowledge gradually and systematically. Another commonplace book is here very useful. In it the student enters every evening, under general headings such as "history" or "philology," what he considers to be the most important new point he has learnt during the day. The entry need not, in fact should not, be lengthy. From six to fifteen lines will generally suffice. The writing out in his own words of what he thinks he knows will often warn the student that his intellectual processes lack definiteness and precision, and at the same time it will impress the memory as nothing else can. A learner cannot realise too early in his career that the test of true knowledge is the power to reproduce. What we read must be assimilated and become a part of our intellectual being. After four years what a useful compilation will have been made, and how active the compiler's mind will have grown in the daily effort to be on the watch for an interesting or valuable insertion!

Pupils even of eighteen or twenty years of age are often surprisingly ignorant of the proper way to use a text-book, and the teacher's advice on this matter will save much time, and avoid much disappointment. A few books have to be mastered, and in such cases an analysis may be necessary. Others, e.g. Zimmern's *Greek Commonwealth*, are read for general ideas, and these ideas must not be vague and hazy, but carefully thought over and expressed in the reader's own words. Thus is gathered excellent material for the commonplace book. The writer once advised a University student, who was completing his course, to revise his Roman history, and suggested that four days would be sufficient, as the subject had already been fully dealt with both in lectures and in private reading. The look of amazement which greeted this suggestion led to a few inquiries, and it was discovered that this man's idea of revision was to re-read two rather bulky text-books. He had no idea of what he knew or of what he did not know. The whole, whether already mastered or not, was to be read over again. The saying of Socrates, that a life without self-examination is no life at all for a human being, received a striking confirmation, and ever since that time the writer has urged his pupils to mark their text-books as they read them for the second time, so that the known may be distinguished from the unknown. If a different mark be used for the portions still unfamiliar upon a third reading, the final revision is a very simple matter indeed.

Sixth-form boys and University students are often, nay usually, very slipshod in their answers to questions on grammar, history and the like. They are apt to follow their text-book, and they rarely show appreciation of evidence and independent judgment. Yet surely it is just these qualities which ought to be developed during a classical course. The writer has often thought that not enough models are put before students. Excellent as our standard editions of the classics undoubtedly are, the notes they contain were not written to discipline the immature mind, but to appeal to trained scholars who can supply the omitted links in the chain of evidence. The best commentator from the educational point of view is almost certainly Bentley, and his edition of Horace has long been a training ground for scholars. But something more modern, and at the same time wider in scope, is very much needed. It has occurred to the writer that a great service would be done for education if a scholar of the first rank, who was not a mere specialist, would write model answers to fifty problems of striking interest in textual criticism, grammar, history, philosophy and archaeology. As far as possible every piece of evidence would be given; *data* would be carefully sifted from inference, and the whole process of reasoning would approximate to syllogistic form. As such a book does not exist, the teacher must perforce supply his pupils with a few models prepared by himself. The strictest application of scientific method to classical studies must be enforced upon even young students if their training is to have a solid and reliable foundation. During a classical course, taste and logical power must be developed side by side.

More thorough and systematic treatment of Greek accents is very desirable. A case could be made out for their entire omission, but the present half-hearted way of dealing with them is thoroughly bad. What could be worse educationally than to scatter accents over an exercise, making perhaps thirty mistakes in the process, merely to make it look more like a printed page? If accents are not wholly discarded, the pupil should be taught what they mean, how they are to be pronounced, and their effect upon reading. A teacher on the direct method finds the accents a great boon. Properly pronounced, they help towards the realisation of the music of the Greek tongue, and this realisation improves a boy's work by profoundly modifying his attitude towards it. A few rules have to be given, but most accents are learnt in the natural manner, that is, by oral practice.

But it is time to turn to the curriculum of the sixth

form and to application of the direct method thereto. It is assumed that about twenty-four periods a week are at our disposal. These will be divided up thus:

Reading of authors	12 periods.
Oral translation	1 period.
Unseen	2 periods.
Correction of work	6 periods.
History and Antiquities ..	3 periods.

Verse composition and unseens have already been dealt with. Prose composition consists, for one year, of summaries of authors read in class with an occasional theme, for the next two years, of ordinary "proses" with an occasional theme. When setting the subject of a theme the master suggests the use of certain constructions, and sometimes of certain idioms; otherwise the range of constructions used is apt to be, at least at first, rather limited. The writer finds that boys often present themes, especially in verse, that they have composed *sua sponte*.

English essays are included in the time given to history. Antiquities form an important, although ancillary, part of the course, and should be closely correlated with the reading of original authorities. There are periodical lessons, and papers, on syntax.

About the reading of authors there is more to be said, for upon it depends the success of the whole course. If a study of the classics is to reach its highest aim, the student must drink deep. Certain books ought to be read in their entirety. Homer, Thucydides, Virgil and Horace belong to this class. One is tempted to add Sophocles, but the amount of drama out of which a selection has to be made renders this impossible, even though Euripides be postponed to the University course as unsuitable for schoolboys. From the other chief classical authors are taken carefully selected portions, and the whole is divided into a cycle of three years. A specimen cycle is given in the next chapter. Some books are reserved for private reading, which does not consist of preparation for class-work, but of the study of authors so reserved and of revision.

Every day two consecutive periods are devoted to reading. The methods adopted are unusual, but their character may be inferred from the specimen which will be given presently. It is now that the direct method reaches its true τέλος, and it is hard to speak, without appearing to exaggerate, of the pleasure and profit each lesson affords. "The greatest care is given to the technique of the reading, rhythm, quantities, accents, and the phrasing in particular. When this is done not only is the meaning clear at once, but new beauties disclose themselves continually. The meaning is clear, because all get into the habit of understanding before they speak; one false grouping, or an intonation that shows want of understanding, and the reader is instantly stopped and bantered until he owns his fault. The fault was, to have spoken before he understood, when he ought to have made sure that he understood before he spoke. The beauties of sound will probably not be credited by those who are content with what passes for reading nowadays....Plain texts are used, and only those notes given which are wanted, not those which may show off the master's knowledge. Parallel passages...are looked up in the form library at once, read and written down or noted; sets of the chief texts are kept there for that purpose. Passages of verse are learnt by heart...but the mere act of reading aloud commits a great deal to the memory without conscious learning." "But it is in the sixth form that this practice [of answering and paraphrasing] becomes most striking. I wish I could show it here as it is; but it is one of those things that pass like a flash and are gone, leaving behind only the impression of pleasure and admiration....It is very difficult to note them down; they come and go so quickly, and the master's attention is fixed on his own work....Often a boy will give a summary off-hand of the last lesson, or of a paragraph just read; or two will discuss the meaning of an argument, or an interpretation, quoting freely from their past reading. At this stage the master's pleasure is at its highest. There is the same sort of charm as in the conversation of a dozen clever men round the mahogany tree. So I give my specimens, reminding readers that they are but the merest scraps, flotsam cast up by the waves, gleanings of the harvest. They are all given exactly as spoken.

Text.	Paraphrase.
Demosthenes *Phil.* III. 51. *ἐκτραχηλισθῆναι.*	(1) *ἀναχαιτισθῆναι.* (2) *λέγεται περὶ ἵππων οἳ καταβάλλουσι τοὺς ἱππέας χαμαί.*
60. *ἀπάγουσιν.*	*ἄνευ δίκης ἄγουσιν ἐς τὸ δεσμωτήριον.*
Sophocles *Electra*, 971. *ἐπαξίων.*	*πρεπόντων.* (One looked puzzled.) *ἐοικότων τινὶ ἀνθρώπῳ.* (Still puzzled.) *ἐὰν ὁ μὲν καλὸς καλῶν γάμων τύχῃ, ὁ δὲ κακὸς κακῶν, ἑκάτερος ἀξίων γάμων τυγχάνει.* (That did it.)[1]"

[1] *Report on the Teaching of Greek at the Perse School*, pp. 36, 30, 31, 32.

Many other specimens are to be found in the *Report*. There follows here a portion of a Latin reading lesson with a sixth form. The author is Horace (*Epistles*). In one double period of one and a half hours it would probably be possible to read from *Epistle* XII to *Epistle* XV of book I. The detailed work on *Epistle* XII is here given, with the omission of certain obvious notes on history and the date of the letter. The boys take down in writing such notes as they think are necessary. If they have been properly trained during the preceding three or four years, they are quite capable of doing this without any elaborate supervision on the part of the master. Each boy reads about fifteen lines, pausing however at every full stop for difficulties to be explained and notes to be taken. In what follows capital letters refer to different boys, *M.* signifying the master.

Fructibus Agrippae Siculis, quos colligis, Icci,
Si recte frueris, non est ut copia maior
Ab Iove donari possit tibi. Tolle querelas:
Pauper enim non est cui rerum suppetit usus.
Si ventri bene, si laterist pedibusque tuis, nil
Divitiae poterunt regales addere maius.
Si forte in medio positorum abstemius herbis
Vivis et urtica, sic vives protinus, ut te
Confestim liquidus Fortunae rivus inauret,
Vel quia naturam mutare pecunia nescit, 10
Vel quia cuncta putas una virtute minora.
Miramur, si Democriti pecus edit agellos
Cultaque, dum peregrest animus sine corpore velox,
Cum tu inter scabiem tantam et contagia lucri
Nil parvum sapias et adhuc sublimia cures:
Quae mare compescant causae, quid temperet annum,

Stellae sponte sua iussaene vagentur et errent,
Quid premat obscurum Lunae, quid proferat orbem,
Quid velit et possit rerum concordia discors,
Empedocles an Stertinium deliret acumen. 20
Verum seu pisces seu porrum et caepe trucidas,
Vtere Pompeio Grospho et siquid petet ultro
Defer: nil Grosphus nisi verum orabit et aequum.
Vilis amicorumst annona, bonis ubi quid deest.
Ne tamen ignores, quo sit Romana loco res:
Cantaber Agrippae, Claudi virtute Neronis
Armenius cecidit; ius imperiumque Phraates
Caesaris accepit genibus minor; aurea fruges
Italiae pleno defundit Copia cornu.

HORACE, *Epp.* I. 12

Lines 1–3.

A. Quis erat Iccius?

B. Amicus Horati et Agrippae minister. Num erat vilicus?

C. Minime. Nonne servi erant vilici? Iccius tamen civis erat qui Agrippae rura custodiebat.

A. Cur "recte"?

E. Nonne recte fruimur fructibus? Ipsa vocabula declarant. "Frui" est verbum, "fructus" nomen.

Line 4.

C. Non intellego sententiam.

A. Is qui utitur aliqua re nihil aliud debet desiderare. Satis est.

M. Recte. Cui datur usus fructuum, is non appellandus est "pauper."

Lines 5, 6.

Nihil est incertum.

10—2

Lines 7–11.

D. Constructio mihi est dubia.

M. Neque mirum. Est enim difficillima. "In medio posita" fortasse significat "volgaria," "communia." Si ita est, arte coniungenda sunt verba cum "abstemius." Sensus erit, "Si communibus ita parce uteris ut vivas herbis et urtica." Alii tamen putant "positorum" significare "appositorum," scilicet ad convivam. Hi sic exponunt, "Si tu abstemius vivis herbis et urtica, etsi pretiosa sunt apposita." Prior explicatio est potior.

E. "Protinus?"

A. "Vives protinus" est "Perges vivere."

F. Quo sensu usurpatur "ut"?

B. "Etsi" valet.

M. Expone undecimum versum.

C. Nullam rem tam valere putas quam virtutem.

Lines 12–20.

C. Significatio me fallit.

A. Iccius magis admirandus est quam Democritus. Hic enim neglexit pecus dum sapientiae studet; ille autem ita rei rusticae studuit ut philosophiam non neglegeret.

M. Recte. "Scabiem tantam et contagia" exemplum est figurae quae *hendiadys* vocatur. "Scabies" est proprie ovium morbus.

C. Quid significat "parvum sapere"?

E. "Nil parvum sapere" est "sublimi sapientiae studere," "sublimia curare," cuius sapientiae in sequentibus versibus exempla inveniuntur.

A. "Temperare annum"?

B. Efficere ut ver, aestas, auctumnus, hiemps recto ordine adveniant.

M. "Obscurum"; scilicet "orbem"; "quid premat orbem lunae ut obscurus sit, quid proferat orbem lunae."

G. "Stertinium acumen"?

M. Acutus Stertinius, qui philosophus erat Stoicus. Empedocles quoque, ut scitis, erat philosophus, qui in Sicilia quinto ante Christum saeculo floruit.

Lines 21–23.

D. Quid significant "porrum" et "caepe"?

E. Herbae sunt, quas edimus; Anglice *leek* et *onion*.

A. Quam mira verba "porrum et caepe trucidas"! Quomodo possumus trucidare herbas?

B. Sed nonne herbae animas habent? Vivunt enim non minus quam nos vivimus.

M. Sic docebat Pythagoras philosophus, qui sine dubio Horatio in mentem venit hunc versum scribenti.

C. Nonne "ultro" hoc loco significat "statim," "sine mora"?

A. Immo, "tua sponte." Da Grospho id quod rogat etiam antequam roget!

Line 24.

G. Non intellego sententiam.

M. "Annona," ut cernis, hoc loco significat "pretium." Si ei, quibus deest aliquid, boni sunt, licet tibi eos parvo pretio amicos facere. Boni enim nihil poscunt nisi verum et aequum, et pro beneficio semper sunt grati.

Lines 25–29.

B. Ex quo dependet "ne tamen ignores"? Valetne modum imperativum?

C. Ellipsis est non ita rara. ⟨Hoc tibi dico⟩ ne ignores.

D. Nonne deest aliquid in versu vicesimo sexto?

F. Ita. Cantaber ⟨cecidit⟩ Agrippae ⟨virtute⟩, Claudi Neronis virtute cecidit Armenius.

A. Cur "Cantaber," singulariter?

B. Simile est:
Tu regere imperio populos, Romane, memento.

C. "Genibus minor"?

A. Nixus genibus, more supplicis[1].

Such is the method, but it can be understood and appreciated only by one who has heard it in practice. The imperfections, the mistakes which are so glaring on the printed page, are felt to be trifles compared with the life of the lesson, its absorbing interest, and its power to bring the mind into real contact with the problems presented by the text. Even the mistakes have their value. Usually they are detected at once—a good sixth form contains sharp critics—and in this way the need for greater care is brought home to all. Continued into the University stage reading classes supplement lectures on special subjects.

CHAPTER IX

THE POSITION OF CLASSICS IN THE CURRICULUM

The old purely classical curriculum, with its many faults and its few virtues, is gone for ever. If the study of classics is to survive, it will be under two conditions:

(1) It must prove its value in modern life, and respond satisfactorily to the supreme test of experience;

[1] This difficult letter should be translated into English, *after* the discussion, so that the master can be sure everything is understood. Usually translation is unnecessary.

(2) It must be thorough, and yet occupy a moderate share of the whole time-table.

The former condition, obviously, cannot be discussed; the latter claims at least a brief notice.

Classical specialists, who hope to pass on to the University, must devote a considerable proportion of their time to Latin and Greek during the last three years of their school life. If the total number of school periods per week is thirty-six, from twenty to twenty-four will be required for classical work. The remaining periods can be given to English, German, French and mathematics.

The two years immediately preceding the period of specialisation demand at least twelve periods per week, six for Greek and six for Latin. During this part of the course the boys may be divided into three groups:

(1) Those who intend to take classics at the University;

(2) Those who intend to proceed to the University, but not as classical students;

(3) Those who are not going to the University at all.

Groups (1) and (2) will take Greek, postponing German until they reach the sixth; group (3) will take German instead of Greek, but will continue their Latin.

During the first two years of the classical course at least six periods per week will be given to Latin, and the boys will be divided, as soon as possible, into two groups:

(1) Potential scholars;

(2) Those who will never do Greek at all.

Bearing in mind the importance of not beginning two languages together, we can now sketch the language course of a boy who is thought likely to profit by the study of at least Latin and possibly of Greek.

Age	Languages
Up to 10	English only.
10–12	English and French, some English periods being dropped.
12–14	English, French and Latin, some English and some French periods being dropped.
14–16	English, French, Latin and Greek or German, more English and French periods being dropped.
16–19	Period of specialisation, German being begun by those who have not taken it before.

Omitting the period of specialisation, we can express the language work in tabular form. Twenty-two periods in all are supposed to be given to languages.

	Periods (per week)			
Age	English	French	Latin	Greek or German
Up to 10	22	—	—	—
10–12	14	8	—	—
12–14	10	6	6	—
14–16	5	5	6	6

Of course "English," during the earlier period of this course, will include much more than the mere study of the English language.

A scheme approximating closely to the above has been in vogue at the Perse School for fourteen years. It is therefore quite workable. But what of the results? The scholarship candidates do very well indeed, both during their school course and at the University. There can be no doubt at all about that point. The same can be said of those who go through the four-year Latin course to the end. But if a boy leaves off Latin after two years, or migrates to another school, the result is somewhat disappointing. A boy learning on the direct method forms ideas which, vague at first, gradually increase in clearness and precision. The full effects of the early work are visible only after a time, and then they are cumulative. It often happens that for two years a boy, though lively and bright, shows no signs of accurate scholarship, and if tested by an examination of the usual type would be pronounced a failure, although he could converse sensibly in Latin or write a short Latin story. And then, suddenly, perhaps in the third year, a change takes place; the effects of the previous teaching appear all at once, and the boy becomes a fair, perhaps a brilliant, success. When a teacher has condemned the direct method, it usually has been because he has examined an immature product by an entirely unsuitable test. The ultimate aim of the new method is the same as that of the old. But the pupils advance along different roads. It is grossly unfair to blame a boy, not because he fails to reach his destination, but because he is not on the other road. If the direct method ever be widely adopted, there must be a radical alteration in the character of our elementary classical examinations.

Latin Curriculum.

Year	Age	Periods per week	Reading	Composition	Grammar	Antiquities
1	12–13	6 (of ¾ hour each)	A first-year course on direct lines	Question and answer Dramatic scenes	Simple sentence	
2	13–14	6	A second-year course on direct lines	Reproduction Plays	Complex sentence	
3	14–15	6–7	*Aeneid*, one book Selections from Livy, Caesar, Horace	Reproduction Summaries Dramatisation Translation	The Period	Outlines of history
4	15–16	6–8	Cicero, *de senectute* and *pro Archia* *Aeneid*, one book Selections from Ovid, Livy, Tacitus	As for third year	Sentence-structure	Outlines continued

Greek Curriculum.

Year	Age	Periods per week	Reading	Composition	Grammar	Antiquities
1	14–15	6	*Greek Boy at Home*	Question and answer Reproduction Translation	Simple and complex sentences	Outlines of history
2	15–16	6	Selections from Lucian, Herodotus, Thucydides, Plato, Homer	Reproduction Summaries Translation	Revision Details filled in	Outlines continued

Course for Sixth Form.

Year	Age	Periods per week	Reading	Composition	Grammar	Antiquities
5–7	16–19	24	Homer, Thucydides, Virgil, Horace Eight dramas (with some Plautus) Herodotus, four books Plato, one or two dialogues Demosthenes, some speeches Selections from Cicero, Lucretius, Livy, Ovid, Tacitus, Juvenal	Summaries Themes Translation Verses (in second year)	Periodical lessons and papers	History Elementary philosophy and archaeology

A cycle of reading for a sixth form.

The time available is assumed to be at least two consecutive periods each day. The books mentioned are those which are actually read in class; no account is taken of private study. This may be used to fill gaps if a term's work cannot be completed, or to read more drama with selections from authors (Catullus, Propertius, etc.) not read in class.

First Year.

Term I. [1]*Odyssey*; Virgil.
Term II. [1]*Iliad;* Cicero (selected works).
Term III. Thucydides I–IV; Livy, three books.

Second Year.

Term I. Herodotus, three or four books; Ovid (selections).
Term II. Drama (three or four Greek plays); Horace *Satires and Epistles.*
Term III. Thucydides V–VIII; Tacitus, four books.

Third Year.

Term I. Drama (three or four Greek plays); Plautus, three plays.
Term II. Plato, one or two dialogues; Horace, some *Odes*, and Cicero (selected works).
Term III. Demosthenes, a few speeches; Juvenal and Lucretius (selections).

[1] Probably not more than half can actually be read in class.

EPILOGUE

No one can write a book on method, no one can even pay a visit to the class-rooms of a good school, without realising how small a part method plays in successful teaching. The strictest following of the most approved rules is of no avail when the master is a nonentity; a magnetic personality can transgress every canon and still produce astounding results. So true it is that the letter kills, while the spirit gives life. The very obviousness of this truth constitutes a danger to education. The fascinating character is certain to be duly appraised, but the value of method, comparatively small though it be, is apt to be unduly depreciated. Conscious of his power, the "born teacher " is only too ready to exercise it without attempting to supplement it in any way. But the State needs, not good teachers only, but the best that can possibly be secured. The personal equation may possibly represent four-fifths of a teacher's value, but the remaining fifth is a factor by no means to be neglected. There is another point to be considered. The value of a method is not a fixed quantity; it varies with the skill the teacher commands, and also with his faith in the plan he is following. Faint-hearted adherents of the direct method are its worst enemies. Their teaching cannot be a success, and their failure is interpreted by critics to be the failure of their cause. But any principle of teaching is powerless to stimulate the learner unless vitalised by a living belief.

The first necessity, then, for success is enthusiastic faith. The second is patience. Few teachers have been trained to speak simple Latin and Greek, and readiness to do so comes only with practice and determination. No long time, however, is required; the habit of excluding English for two or three hours a day produces wonderful results in a week or two. Colleagues can give mutual assistance by conversing in an ancient tongue for half-an-hour every evening. Progress will be rapid, especially if attention be paid to distinct articulation and care be taken to pronounce the vowels accurately and with correct quantity. Very soon no practice will be required beyond that afforded by the class-room. And perseverance will bring a rich reward. New beauties will be seen in the ancient authors, and a juster appreciation will be felt of their powers of expression. The writer can bear witness to this from his own personal experience. The sense of power, of mastery over the languages, is so increased that the teacher's efficiency grows apace.

The direct method demands brightness and vivacity. It is constantly calling upon the teacher's capacity to interest his class, to seize any chance opportunity afforded by an incident in the lesson of driving home a new point, to connect the work with the reality of a boy's experience. If he can sketch on the black-board, so much the better. He must develop to the full any dramatic talent he may possess. His most deadly sin and his greatest danger lie in being dull.

Scholarship also is of great importance, but it must be real scholarship, not mere erudition. The essential thing is educated taste, the power to distinguish correct from incorrect idiom, and to banish dubious expressions until fuller knowledge has rejected or confirmed them.

It is unlikely that any teacher, certainly no teacher gifted with initiative and independence, will agree with all the details of method given in this book. It would be a pity if he did, even though he assented to the main principles of the direct method. Any supporter worth having is bound to modify procedure so as to adapt principles to the peculiarities of his own personality. The details of this book are intended merely to be suggestive, to be testimony to what has already been found useful, by some teachers at least, in actual class teaching. But if others who are in substantial agreement with the fundamental principle, that a language is best learnt without the intervention of the mother tongue, shall hereafter develop more successful means of applying it, nobody will be more grateful than he who offers to the public this record of his experience. Only let the ultimate aim of every classical teacher never be obscured. Whether he is dealing with ancient life or with the languages which are the expression of that life, his guiding principle should be so to instil a knowledge of the past as to create a fuller appreciation of the present, and a more rational anticipation of the future.

APPENDIX

UNCORRECTED SPECIMENS OF WORK DONE BY BOYS

1. *Second Year Latin* (*reproduction*).

Olim puer senem quendam, qui iter faciebat, iaciendis lapidibus lacessivit. Senex igitur cum ut desisteret frustra precatus esset aliquantulum pecuniae ei dedit, dixitque se paenitere quod plus non haberet; monstravit tamen divitiorem quendam viatorem qui a tergo appropinquabat, puerumque monuit ut maioris praemii accipiendi causa lapides in eum quoque iaceret. Cuius praecepta secutus simul atque alter viator advenit in eum quoque lapides iecit. Sed tantum afuit ut viator salutis causa pecuniam praeberet ut servos suos ad magistratum illum ducere iuberet, maximasque poenas dedit puer.

2. *First Year Greek* (*reproduction*).

ὁ πίθηκος ζῷόν ἐστιν ὥσπερ καὶ ἄνθρωπος, ἀλλὰ μικρότερον. ἔχει τὰς κόμας ἐπὶ τοῦ προσώπου, καὶ δόλιον βλέπει. ἐσθίει τὰ κάρυα καὶ τὸ ἔξω ἐκβάλλει. διδάσκομεν αὐτὸν χορεύειν, καὶ αὐλεῖν. ἂν μὴ διδακτὸς ᾖ τοὺς ἀνθρώπους μιμῆται. τροφός τις παιδίον ἔλουε ἐν τῇ σκάφῃ. ἔπειτα δὲ τίθησι τὸ παιδίον χαμαὶ ἐν ἐρημίᾳ καὶ ἀποχωρεῖ. ἀποχωρησάσης τῆς τροφοῦ ὁ πίθηκος θρώσκει ἐν τὴν οἰκίαν καὶ λύει τὰ σπάργανα τοῦ παιδίου. φεῦ, τίθησι τὸ παιδίον ἐν ὕδωρ θημότατον, καὶ εὐθὺς ἀποθνῄσκει τὸ παιδίον.

3. *Exordium and peroration of a Latin speech by a boy in his fourth year of Latin.*

Mihi, patres conscripti, qui pro multis saepe dixi, nonnullis saluti in periculis ac discriminibus fui, in principem quem omnes populi, omnes reges, et patres et liberi ipsi oderunt, cuius ferocitate oppressi et togati et milites, a quo, cum aedes, et urbes destructae, tum infantes et mulieres interfectae sunt, in hunc, patres conscripti, orationem habere necesse est; quod nisi ne impune poenam meritam evitaret exemplumque crudelitatis posteritati traderet, timerem, facere vix possem. Si quis ex vobis patrem amisit, si quis filium, si quis fratrem, at credo neminem adesse qui non amiserit, si quis templa domusque ruentes et decidentes vidit, vel matres ex domibus expulsas, atque ruentibus inter ruinas Germanos barbaros maledicere, si quis haec vidit, in hoc monstrum referenda sunt omnia.

Principem capitis reum non mos est mihi vehementer accusare, quod est crudelis hominis, non clementis; sed tamen qui factis suis humanitatis ac probitatis nomen repudiavit, is severitate non clementia dignus est. Humanitatem! Hoc enim nomine in omnibus factis ac dictis, in omni ferocitate, in omnibus cladibus se excusavit, ita enim ut nunc "Humanitas Germanica" apud nos proverbium sit. Sed haec omnia, patres conscripti, modo in memoriam vobis revoco; antea certe scivistis; tamen quia non bene quod iam factum est animo concipere et intellegere possumus, ut diligenter mihi attendatis precor, ita ut omnia quae narro iterum ante oculos ponere possitis; ut haec mihi concedatis precor. At ne quis forte miretur me ita dicere, tanto animo atque vi hunc accusare, tantopere commoveri, ne quis me crudelem et iniustum esse arbitretur, quod quem antea omnes reges, omnes populi, magno honore ornaverunt, atque gravem, constantem, probum iudicaverunt, eum profligatum, crudelissimum, scelestum nunc dico, ne quis hac suspicione percussus me hominem innocentem calumniari velle reatur, crimina breviter exponam. Nam hic non iustum bellum iniuste gessit, sed iniustum crudeliter atque iniuriose. Parva videtur esse tanti belli causa.

De exploratoribus imperatores nostri et homines principes, ne plebem, qui rumores modo audiebat, perturbarent et terrerent, nihil nuntiaverunt; qui tamen exploratorum facta inspiciebant, qui multos ceperunt, epistulasque et chartas in quibus ad Caesarem principem de rebus nostris militaribus nuntia mittere conati sunt, secrete abstulerunt, hi principem illum multos huc misisse non erant nescii. In his quoque epistulis talia inveniebantur ut alios capere et damnare possemus, quorum unum a militibus nostris capitis esse damnatum omnes sciunt. Cum de hoc Germani audivissent, iniustum esse dixerunt, qua excusatione usi aliquos ex imperatoribus nostris quos ceperant in vincula iecerunt, qui omnes labores subibant, omnes indignitates contumeliasque perferre coacti sunt, pauci etiam fame perierunt. Aliqui tamen nos eodem modo captivis Germanicis usos arguunt. Germani nostris omnem indignitatem et crudelitatem imposuerunt, nos non modo non eis male usi sumus, vero etiam liberaliter ac benigne eos habuimus, et qui ordine digni essent honore affecimus. Aliis Germanicis captivis, quos facta abominanda commisisse certum est, severitate aliquando, crudelitate autem numquam usi sumus. Sed ne hos quidem castigare voluimus, ne homines qui iussis modo imperatorum parebant, quae perficere recusare non poterant, iniure puniremus. Hic igitur omnes det poenas, ab hoc qui barbaris suis iussa immania ac terribilia dabat, eas sumere necesse est. Quod si homines non facient, di certe qui fletus mulierum et infantum audiverunt, qui bestiae ferocitatem in degeneris hominis corpore, turpis hominis astutia praeditam nec ullis crudelitatis factis satiatam viderunt, hunc punient. Vos oro, patres conscripti, ne omnes qui in bello pro patria, pro liberis, pro religione, pro populorum libertate, pro totius denique orbis terrarum salute suscepto, impavidi perierunt, inultos esse sinatis, ut morientum supplicibus, viduarum et lugentium vocibus aures adferatis, ut hunc qui ne bellum dicam, latrocinium enim potius quam bellum nominaretur, tam crudeliter gerebat, poenas meritas ac iustas solvere cogatis.

4. *Sixth Form Work.*

(*a*) Summary.

Φίλιππος, ὁ τῶν Μακεδόνων βασιλεύς, ὢν τὸ κατ' ἀρχὰς ἀσθενὴς μετ' ὀλίγον χρόνον ἐπιφέρων πόλεμον ἀεὶ ταῖς ὁμόροις πόλεσι οὕτως μέγας ἐγένετο ὥστε φόβον παρέχειν ἐνίοις καὶ τῶν Ἀθηναίων μή ποτε ἐς τὰς Ἀθήνας βαδίζοι.

οἱ Ὀλύνθιοι σύμμαχοι μὲν τὸ πρῶτον ὄντες τοῦ Φιλίππου, ἐχθροὶ δὲ ὕστερον γεγενημένοι διὰ τὸ ἄπιστον εἶναι αὐτὸν, πρέσβειαν ἔπεμψαν ἐς τὰς Ἀθήνας, ὅτε ὁ Φίλιππος δηλὸς ἐγένετο πολιορκήσων τὴν πόλιν, ἥτις ἐρεῖ τ' αὐτοῖς τὰ πεπραγμένα καὶ ἀξιώσει βοηθεῖν τοῖς Ὀλυνθίοις. ὁ μὲν οὖν Δημοσθένης πείθειν πειρᾶται τοὺς Ἀθηναίους στράτευμά τε παρασκευάζεσθαι καὶ αὐτοὺς ἐξελθεῖν. οὗτοι γὰρ ξένοις ἐχρῶντο πρὸς τὸ πολεμεῖν τοὺς πολέμους οὐδὲ οὕτως πρόθυμοι ἦσαν ὡς προσῆκεν ἐς τὸ ἀντιλάβεσθαι τῶν πραγμάτων.

λέγει δ' ὁ Δημοσθένης ὅτι διχῇ βοηθητέον ἐστὶ τοῖς πράγμασιν, τῷ τε στρατιώτας καὶ ναῦς ἐκπέμψαι ἐς τὴν Ὄλυνθον, καὶ τῷ ἄλλους ἐκπέμψαι κακῶς ποιήσοντας τὴν τοῦ Φιλίππου· ἐπεὶ ἐὰν μὲν μόνον ἐς τὴν Ὄλυνθον βοηθῶσιν, ἀσφαλῶς ἔχοντα τὰ οἴκοι ὁρῶν μείζονι προθυμίᾳ ἐπεῖσιν ὁ Φίλιππος ἐπὶ τὴν πόλιν, ἐὰν δὲ μόνον κακῶς ποιῶσι τὴν αὐτοῦ, ἀνεχόμενος ταῦτα, χρόνῳ παραστήσεται τοὺς Ὀλυνθίους. καὶ δὴ καὶ λέγει ὅτι μάλιστα δεῖ τοὺς Ἀθηναίους ἀνταίρειν τῷ Φιλίππῳ ἐπεὶ ἐὰν νῦν ῥαθυμῶσι τέλος καὶ ἐν τῇ οἰκείᾳ δεήσει αὐτοὺς πολεμεῖν.

ὕστερον δὲ δείκνυσιν ὁ Δημοσθένης ὅτι ἀπατῶν πάντας ηὐξήθη ὁ Φίλιππος καὶ ὅτι ἐὰν καιρὸν ἔχοντες νῦν ἐρρωμένως βοηθῶσι τοῖς Ὀλυνθίοις οἱ Ἀθηναῖοι, σφαλοῦσι μετ' ὀλίγον τὴν αὐτοῦ δύναμιν οὐκ ἀληθῶς βέβαιαν οὖσαν.

DEMOSTHENES, *Olynthiac* I. and II. 1–10.

(*b*) Translation into English.

So I adhere to my opinion and wonder that some people should re-open the question of the Mitylenians and cause a delay which is chiefly to the advantage of those in the wrong (for the injured party then attacks the offenders with his anger blunted, and when vengeance follows the hardest on the footsteps of injury then it is that it is adequate and takes satisfaction the better), and I wonder who will oppose and undertake to show that while our misfortunes are harmful to our allies, the crimes of the Mitylenians are useful to us. It is clear he would either trust to his eloquence and try to show that the resolution we took was not decided on, or he would have been bribed and would try to seduce you by an elaborate and specious argument. The State in such contests gives prizes to others but herself takes the risk. For this you are to blame for making bad conditions; you listen to speeches like spectators in a theatre, you take facts by hearsay, you take your ideas as to the possibilities of the future from clever speeches, you do not consider as any surer that which has taken place before your very eyes than that which you have heard from a cleverly-worded invective.

You are fit men to be deceived by the novelty of an argument, you prefer not to follow what you have approved, you are slaves of every new paradox and despisers of the ordinary, in that each of you would like to speak himself, and if that is impossible, you all vie with those of your own opinion in not appearing to lag behind in insight, you wish to applaud when the speaker says something clever even before he has got it out, you are eager to perceive beforehand what is being said and slow to see that which follows; you seek something different from the world in which we live; in short you are overcome by the pleasures of the ear and are more like men sitting at a display of sophists than men taking counsel for the public good.

THUCYDIDES, III. 38.

(*c*) Greek Verse.

For Greek Iambics.

DUKE. Now my co-mates and brothers in exile,
Hath not old custom made this life more sweet
Than that of painted pomp? Are not these woods
More free from peril than the envious court?
Here feel we but the penalty of Adam,
The season's difference; as the icy fang
And churlish chiding of the winter's wind,
Which when it bites and blows upon my body,
Even till I shrink with cold, I smile and say
"This is no flattery: these be counsellors
That feelingly persuade me what I am."

As You Like It, II. i.

ἄγε νυν ἕταιροι συζυγέντες ὧδε μοι
—σύν μοι φυγόντες ὥστε φαίνεσθαι κάσεις,
ἐνταῦθ' ἐν ὕλαις νῦν βιοῦν εἰώθαμεν·
κᾆρ' οὐ βιοῦν ὧδ' ἥδιον μάλ' ἢ τὸ πρὶν
ἐν τοῦ τυράννου ταῖς θύραις ψεύδους πλέαις;
ἐνταῦθα γὰρ συμπάντες εἰσ' ἐλεύθεροι·
ἀλλ' ἔνθα δεινόν ἐστι πᾶν ὄντος φθόνου.
ἡμεῖς δὲ δεινὸν οὐδὲν ὧδε πάσχομεν,
εἰ μὴ καλεῖ τις τήνδε τὴν πάντων τύχην,
χειμῶνας ὄμβρους ἄλλα τοιαῦτα, φίλοι.
ψυχρῶς γὰρ ἐσθ' ὅτ' ὠμὸς ὢν βορρᾶς πικρὸς
πρός σῶμα μου πνεῖ χὤστ' ἀποῤῥιγοῦν κρύει·
παθὼν δὲ τοῦτ' ἐγώγε μειδιῶν λέγω·
"βορρᾶς ἀληθής ἐστιν, οὐχὶ θωψ ἐμοί·
"πρόβουλος οἷος εἰμι δείκνυσιν καλῶς·
"οὔκ εἰμι γὰρ θεός τις, ἀσθενὴς δ' ἀνήρ."

(Third piece attempted.)

For Greek Iambics.

CÆSAR. The night grows on, and you are for your meeting;
I'll therefore end in few. Be resolute,
and put your enterprise in act; the more
actions of depth and danger are consider'd,
the less assuredly they are perform'd:
and thence it happeneth, that the bravest plots,
not executed straight, have been discover'd.
Say, you are constant, or another, a third,
or more; there may be yet one wretched spirit,
with whom the fear of punishment shall work
'bove all the thoughts of honour and revenge.
You are not now to think what's best to do,
as in beginnings; but, what must be done,
being thus enter'd; and slip no advantage
that may secure you. Let 'em call it mischief:
when it is past, and prosper'd, 'twill be virtue.
They're petty crimes are punish'd, great rewarded.
Nor must you think of peril, since attempts
begun with danger, still do end with glory;
and, when need spurs, despair will be call'd wisdom.
Less ought the care of men, or fame to fright you,
for they that win do seldom receive shame
of victory, howe'er it be achieved,
and vengeance, least: for who, besieged with wants,
would stop at death, or anything beyond it?
Come, there was never any great thing yet
aspiréd, but by violence or fraud:
and he that sticks, for folly of a conscience,
to reach it—

CATILINE. Is a good religious fool. B. JONSON.

CÆSAR. *νῦν δ' ἔρχεται νὺξ καὶ ποθεῖτε συμβαλεῖν·*
ὡς συνταμεῖν οὖν εἰς τέλος φράσω τόσον.
ἔργων χρέων νῦν· δράσατ' εὐτόλμως τὸ πᾶν.
ὅσῳ πλέον γὰρ δεινὸν ἔργον ᾖ μέγα
γνώμῃ σκοπεῖτε χρώμενοι, τόσῳ πλέον
ὀκνεῖσθε δρῶντες· ὥστε καὶ καλοὺς δόλους

οὐκ εὐθὺς ἐκπραχθέντας ἐξέφηνέ τις.
καὶ δὴ βέβαιος οὗτος ἢ κεῖνος· τί οὖν;
ἴσως γὰρ εἶς τις ἄλλος ὃς δείδων δίκην
ἐκλήσεται τίμης τε καὶ τιμωρίας.
οὐ δεῖ τὸ δόξαν ὥσπερ ἄρχοντας σκοπεῖν
ἀλλ' ὡς ἀφορμήσαντες ἐκπράσσειν τάχα,
λίθον τε κινεῖν πάντα πρὸς τὸ τυγχάνειν.
ἡμᾶς καλούντων νῦν κακούς· ἀλλ' ὕστερον
πᾶσιν φανούμεθ' εὐτυχήσαντες καλοί.
ὅστις κακουργεῖ φαῦλ' ἀεὶ τίνει δίκην,
ἀλλ' οὗτος ὅστις μέγαλα, τιμᾶται πολύ.
καὶ μὴ τὸ δεινὸν ἐκφοβεῖσθ'· ἅπας ἀγὼν
δεινὸς τὸ πρῶτον εἰς τέλος τίμην ἔχει.
μηδ' ἐκφοβεῖσθε δόξαν ἀνθρώπων κακήν·
ὁ γὰρ κρατήσας οὔποτ' αἰσχύνην ἔχει
νίκης, κεχρημένος περ αἰσχίστοις δόλοις·
μηδ' ἐκφοβεῖσθε μηδαμῶς τιμωρίαν·
πάσχοντ' ἀπορίαν πανταχοῦ τίν' ἂν ποτε
φόβος κατίσχοι τοῦ μόρου τοῦ θ' Ἅιδου;
ἄγε νῦν· τί πρᾶγμα μηχανώμενον μέγα
οὐκ ἐξεπράχθη μηχάναισι καὶ βίᾳ;
ὅστις δὲ μῶρος τοῦδ' ἀποκνοίη θεοὺς
φοβούμενός πως οὗτος—

CATILINE. εὐσεβεῖ μάτην.

Swifter far than summer's flight,
Swifter far than youth's delight,
Swifter far than happy night,
Art thou come and gone.

As the earth when leaves are dead,
As the night when sleep is sped,
As the heart when joy is fled,
I am left lone, alone.

Lilies for a bridal bed,
Roses for a matron's head,
Violets for a maiden dead.
Pansies let my flowers be.

On the living grave I bear
Scatter them without a tear,
Let no friend however dear,
Waste one hope, one fear for me.

SHELLEY.

ὠκύπους ὥρα θέρεος παρεῖσι,
ὠκύπους δ' ἄβας χάρις, ὠκύπους δὲ
νὺξ μακαίρα. τῶνδε σὺ θᾶσσον, ἐλθοῖσ',
αἶψ' ἀποφεύγεις.

ὡς δὲ γᾶ φύλλων δίχα καππεσόντων,
ἠὲ νὺξ, ὅτ' ἄδυς ἄπεστιν ὕπνος,
ἦ κέναι τέρψεως φρένες, ὧδ' ἐρῆμος
ἔμμι, μονωθείς.

νυμφίω λέχεος κρίνα, ματέρων τε
ἄνθε' ἄδιστα βρόδα καὶ θανοίσας
εὖ πρέπει κόρας ἴα· νῦν γὰρ ἔστω
μοι κυπάρισσος.

πενθίμων πεδ' ἔμμι νέκρων, βίους περ·
λίσσομαι δὲ, σπέρρ', ἄδακρυς τὰ φῦλλα.
ἐλπίδας γὰρ φάμι δέος τε κούφαις
ἔμμεναι ὔμμιν.

GOD SAVE THE KING.

ΣΚΟΛΙΟΝ.

ἔρχομαί σε θεῶν ἄνακτα κἀνδρῶν
τῆσδε λισσόμενος πόλεως τυράννῳ
βίοτον πορεῖν μακρότερον,
κῦδος ἀναίτιον καὶ στέφανον κράτους.

τοὺς ἐχθροὺς σκεδάσας βολαῖς κεραυνοῦ
σῶσον, ὦ βασιλεῦ, τύραννον ἡμῖν,
κακοτεχνίας σφάλλε πρόπαν
ὠφελίαν τε δὸς πᾶσι παραστάτης.

ἀλλὰ τῷ βασιλεῖ μέγιστ' ὄπαζε
δῶρά τ' ἔκκριτα καὶ βίον πάνολβον,
ἵνα τοῖς πολίταις παρέχῃ
ἀθανάτους ἔχειν θεσμία καὶ νόμους.

(*d*) Greek Prose.

For Greek Prose.

EUPHRANOR.—LYSICLES.

EUPH. Say, Lysicles, who drinks most, a sick man or a healthy?

LYS. A healthy.

EUPH. And which is healthiest, a sober man or a drunkard?

LYS. A sober man.

EUPH. A sober man therefore in health may drink more than a drunkard when he is sick.

LYS. He may.

EUPH. What think you, will a man consume more meat and drink in a long life or a short one?

LYS. In a long.

EUPH. A sober, healthy man, therefore, in a long life may circulate more money by eating and drinking, than a glutton or drunkard in a short one.

LYS. What then?

EUPH. Why then it should seem, that he may be more beneficial to the public even in this way of eating and drinking.

LYS. I shall never own that temperance is the way to promote drinking.

EUPH. But you will own that sickness lessens, and death puts an end to all drinking. The same argument will hold for aught I can see, with respect to all other vices that impair men's health and shorten their lives.

BERKELEY, *Minute Philosopher*, Dialogue 2.

Εὐφ. εἰπέ μοι, ὦ Λυσίκλεις· πότερον φῂς πλέον πίνειν, τὸν νοσοῦντα ἢ τὸν ὑγιαίνοντα;

Λυσ. τὸν νοσοῦντα δήπου.

Εὐφ. πότερος δὲ πλέον ὑγιαίνει, ὁ μετριοπότης ἢ ὁ οἰνόφλυξ;

Λυσ. ὅ γε μετριοπότης, νὴ τὸν Δία.

Εὐφ. εἰκὸς ἄρ' ἐστι τὸν μετριοπότη, ἐν ᾧ ἂν ὑγιαίνῃ, πλέον πίνειν τοῦ οἰνόφλυγος νοσοῦντος;

Λυσ. εἰκὸς, ὦ Εὐφράνωρ.

Εὐφ. φέρε τοίνυν· τί σοι δοκεῖ; πότερον μακρὸν βιώσας τις βίον ἢ καὶ βραχὺν, πλέον φαγεῖταί τε καὶ πίεται;

Λυσ. βραχὺν, εἰκότως.

Εὐφ. ὁ οὖν μετριοπότης ἅμα ὑγιαίνων, ἐὰν μακρὸν βιώσῃ βίον, πλέον ἂν εἰκότως δαπανήσειεν ἀργύριον ἢ ἀδηφάγος τέ τις καὶ οἰνόφλυξ βίον βιώσας βραχύν;

Λυσ. τί δαί, ὦ Εὐφράνωρ;

Εὐφ. ὅτι ἔμοιγε δοκεῖ ἐκεῖνος διὰ ταῦτα καὶ πλέον ἂν ὠφελῆσαι τοῖς πολίταις ὧδε ἐσθίων τε καὶ πίνων.

Λυσ. οὐδεπώποτε, ὦ Εὐφράνωρ, ἐκεῖνο ὁμολογήσομαι, ὅτι μετρίως ἐσθίων τέ τις καὶ πίνων ποιεῖ ὥστε πλέονας γενέσθαι τοὺς οἰνόφλυγας.

Εὐφ. ἀλλὰ μήν, ὦγαθέ, ἐκεῖνό γε δήπου ὁμολογεῖς, ὅτι τὸ μὲν νοσεῖν ὀλίγον τι τὸ πίνειν ἀποπαύει, ὁ δὲ θάνατος παντελῶς. οὕτω τοίνυν καὶ περὶ πάσης τῆς ἀκολασίας (ἔμοιγε δοκεῖν) ἔχει, δι' ἣν ἔλαττόν τε ὑγιαίνουσιν οἱ ἄνθρωποι καὶ βραχίονα ἔχουσι τὸν βίον.

(*e*) Latin verse.

For Latin Elegiacs.

No blustering wind did shake the shady trees,
Each leaf lay still and silent in the wood,
The birds were musical, the labouring bees
That in the summer heap the winter's good,
Plied to their hives sweet honey from those flowers,
Whereout the serpent strengthens all his powers.

The lion laid and stretcht him in the lawns,
No storm did hold the leopard from his prey,
The fallow fields were full of wanton fawns,
The plow-swains never saw a fairer day,
For every beast and bird did take delight
To see the quiet heavens to shine so bright.

ROBERT GREENE.

Non agitant ramos strepitantia flamina opacos;
  Frondibus immotis silva quieta iacet.
Dum cantant volucres, apium nunc turba laborat;
  Sic aestate solent accumulare cibum.
Firmatur coluber, vires e floribus augens,
  Ast apis ex illis aurea mella legit.

A praedis pardum tempestas nulla coercet;
  Corpore nunc pressit gramina picta leo.
Iam simul est haedis lascivis plena novalis;
  Miratur pulchram rustica turba diem.
Omnia per terram cernunt animalia laete
  Quam liquido caeli lumine templa micent.

These exercises are printed without corrections, in order to show:

(*a*) results actually achieved;

(*b*) the common types of error met with by the "direct" teacher.

They are quite ordinary specimens, not show pieces. The writer of (3), however, is a very gifted boy, and his work is much above the average.

BIBLIOGRAPHY

Board of Education Reports:

(1) *The Teaching of Classics in Secondary Schools in Germany.*

(2) *The Teaching of Latin at the Perse School, Cambridge.*

(3) *The Teaching of Greek at the Perse School, Cambridge.*

Latin Teaching, the Journal of the Association for the Reform of Latin Teaching, editor Mr C. L. Mainwaring, 26 Sydenham Road, Croydon.

Praeceptor, S. O. Andrew. (Oxford University Press.)

Some Practical Suggestions on the Direct Method of Teaching Latin, R. B. Appleton. (Heffer.)

The Teaching of Latin, W. H. S. Jones. (Blackie.)

INDEX

For EU product safety concerns, contact us at Calle de José Abascal, 56–1°, 28003 Madrid, Spain or eugpsr@cambridge.org.

www.ingramcontent.com/pod-product-compliance
Ingram Content Group UK Ltd.
Pitfield, Milton Keynes, MK11 3LW, UK
UKHW012343130625
459647UK00009B/494

* 9 7 8 1 1 0 7 6 2 3 1 4 9 *